Mountains and Rainbows

USSR
CANADA
Prudhoe Bay
PIPELINE
ARCTIC
CIRCLE
Eagle
Nome
Fairbanks
Dawson City
Delta Jct.
Tok
ALASKA HWY.
DENALI PARK
Palmer
Whitehorse
Anchorage
Valdez
Skagway
Kenai Peninsula
Juneau
Kodiak

Mountains and Rainbows

Modern pioneers - how Alaska changed their lives

10/5/91

To—
Annabell
Enjoy—
Best wishes—
Have fun in Alaska ——
Ardyce

Ardyce Czuchna-Curl
Photographs by the author

Oak Woods Media, Inc.

Library of Congress Cataloging-in-Publication Data

Czuchna-Curl, Ardyce, 1934-
Mountains and rainbows : modern pioneers, how Alaska changed their lives / Ardyce Czuchna-Curl.
Includes index.
ISBN 0-88196-002-0 : $16.95. — ISBN 0-88196-001-2 (pbk.) : $9.95
1. Alaska—Description and travel—1981- 2. Alaska—Social life and customs. 3. Czuchna-Curl, Ardyce, 1934- —Journeys—Alaska. 4. Pioneers—Alaska—Interviews. I. Title.
F910.5.C96 1989 89-3079
979.8'05 CIP

ISBN 0-88196-002-0 Cloth
ISBN 0-88196-001-2 Pbk

Printed in the United States of America

Published by Oak Woods Media, Inc.
PO Box 527
Oshtemo, MI 49077
(616) 375-5621

To Dave, without whom this book
would not have happened

Acknowledgements:

Thanks to Dave Curl, my husband, for editorial and photographic help.

Thanks to Aletha Lindstrom, Maris Soule, Marie Latta, Jane Vander Weyden and Pat Kline for encouragement, suggestions and critical reading.

Thanks, too, to other members of the Battle Creek Free Lance Writers, Michigan Press Women and National Federation of Press Women who patiently listened and offered suggestions.

Thanks also to Alex Ellingsen, who introduced me to the world of desktop publishing.

Special thanks to the individuals who shared their stories. Many of these interviews have appeared as feature articles in *The Kalamazoo Gazette, The Grand Rapids Press, The Battle Creek Enquirer* and *Michigan Farmer* magazine.

This book was created electronically on an Apple® Macintosh® II computer using Microsoft® Word 3.0 and Aldus® PageMaker® 3.0. The map was prepared with Aldus® FreeHand™ 2.0. Printed on a QMS-PS® 810 laser printer.

Mountains and Rainbows

Modern pioneers - how Alaska changed their lives

Foreword

Frontiers attract the fearless, the curious, the restless, the bold. They come into the country, these adventurers, some seeking excitement, others searching for solitude. A few find the kind of "gold" they thought they were looking for. Some pack up and leave, disillusioned and empty-handed. But many who return to where they came from and most who remain on the frontier finish out their lives oddly enobled.

The survivors carry forever the pride of having tested themselves and passed; they savor the satisfaction of having accomplished something greater than they had ever imagined.

Those who dare to accept the challenge presented by the Land of the Midnight Sun seldom remain strangers there. As we traveled three times to and through America's largest state, my husband Dave and I were accepted instantly by people who preceded us, who shared the bond of seeking and survival. We asked Alaskans, "Why did you come to this land?"

They asked us only, "Where are you from?"

We were warmly welcomed in Alaska, and we always felt as if we belonged there. One tourist brochure said, "Once you've been to Alaska, you never go all the way home." We did come home, but we brought with us memories of places and people we can never forget.

We would remember the remote village of Chicken. Here we met Ann Purdy who arrived in the Alaskan wilderness as a young schoolteacher 50 years earlier. Here she met her husband-to-be and now lives out her life as a widow hoping visitors will see the hand-lettered signs, come to her cabin, buy an autographed copy of *Tisha,* the story of her adventuresome life, and chat awhile about the old days.

We would drive across the Arctic Circle on the formidable North Slope Haul Road (now named the Dalton Highway). We would fly to Prudhoe Bay in the winter, and receive a grand tour of the headquarters and drilling sites of SOHIO escorted by Dana Stabenow, information services coordinator for the oil company. Touring the North Slope at -40 degrees F was something like being in outer space. The completely self-contained complex of living quarters, offices and recreational and dining facilities made us feel as if we were orbiting the Earth on board a manned space station.

Visiting the state museum in Juneau fed our minds; hiking the nearby Mendenhall Glacier nourished our spirits; and frequenting salmon bakes just outside Alaska's rainy capital satisfied our stomachs.

As we traveled around the state in midsummer when it never really gets dark, we marveled at the midnight sun as children played outside at 11 p. m. and people chatted with friends and worked on projects until early morning hours.

"We sleep in the winter," explained Neil Schenk, a dairy farmer near Delta Junction. During the long nights of winter, Neil's wife Pat creates artwork to sell in local gift shops and to display in their own home. We arrived at the Schenks' farm one warm July evening at nine o'clock for an interview and remained there until midnight.

Before our odyssey was finished, in three journeys spanning five years, we would have driven nearly every connected highway in Alaska and interviewed more than a hundred people. Each one had a story to tell.

Arriving as cheechakos—having yet to endure the sourdough's initiation of remaining warm and dry through an arctic winter—it seemed to us in the first summer that we already belonged in the North, and that in this remote, beautiful country, a part of us would always remain. If we chose, we could stay here as others had done, creating a new life together.

As children we had seen the North only through the eyes of imagination, but we had felt it—the irresistible pull—the lure of The Great Land; Robert Service called it *The Spell of the Yukon:**

"...There's the land. (Have you seen it?)
    It's the cussedest land that I know,
From the big, dizzy mountains that screen it
    To the deep, deathlike valleys below.
Some say God was tired when He made it;
    Some say it's a fine land to shun;
Maybe; but there's some as would trade it
    For no land on earth—and I'm one."

---

* *The Best of Robert Service* (Toronto: McGraw-Hill Ryerson, 1963).

The Highway

The thick, red dust was settling in my throat and I could hardly swallow. I was beginning to have second thoughts about my first trip to Alaska. Already my hair felt greasy and my eyes burned. Dave is driving too fast, I thought, as the truck rattled and bumped into each pothole and careened on the loose gravel around sudden curves, unprotected by guard rails.

The shoulder belt cut into my chest and jerked me as Dave jammed on the brakes and wrestled the steering wheel to swerve around a camper rig like ours—lying wheels up in the middle of the narrow right-of-way.

Although the occupants were unharmed, their possessions were strewn over the highway. They were picking up the pieces. Dear God, I thought. This might happen to us on the next curve! It was another 1,500 miles to Fairbanks. And who wanted to go to Fairbanks anyway?

We had left Dawson Creek, British Columbia, Milepost "0" of the Alaska Highway that morning. The highway, built by the U. S. Army Corps of Engineers in the 1940's, had been featured in a little paper called *My Weekly Reader* and I still

The milepost "0" sign greets travelers at Dawson Creek, British Columbia

remembered it from grade school. Built cooperatively by the Canadian and U. S. governments, the hastily constructed highway—at that time referred to as the "Alcan"—was a military supply route for our Alaskan outposts and an overland lifeline, safe from the wartime hazards of shipping.

The highway opened in March 1942 after eight months of frenzied construction activity spurred by fear of a Japanese invasion that never materialized. After the war, the narrow, rutted mud road was turned over to civilian contractors with the idea that the right-of-way would be widened and graveled, the most abrupt curves straightened, and the primitive bridges replaced with steel structures.

The Alaska Highway has never been completed even after more than 40 years, although much of it is now paved, and the road is constantly being improved and repaired to keep up with damage caused by constant freezing and thawing and heavier traffic each year.

The history was fascinating, yet right then and there I wanted to go home—to leave this damnable stretch of wasteland. I was scared. "Turn back!" I wanted to cry.

But I didn't. No. I couldn't tell Dave I was chicken. Perhaps I could try a soft approach, "Honey, I've been thinking about it and since this is such hard driving for you, why don't we take the ferry up from Prince Rupert?"

No, that wouldn't work. We both knew that reservations

were all booked up and one of the ferries was out of commission. I would stick it out. Besides, I knew Dave really wanted to conquer the Alcan—all the way.

Thousands of people travel this rough road every year; but partly because of the legends of the past, it's still considered a macho thing to earn a bumper sticker that reads: "I survived the Alcan Highway."

I loved Dave—cared about him enough to do with him what he wanted to do. So I closed my eyes and tried to relax. Maybe it would get better. I breathed deeply and tried to think of something else.

There had been other fears. Years ago when my first child was on the way, I was scared—anticipating labor pains and the birth ordeal. But then I told myself, "Look at all of the millions of women who have given birth and survived. If they did it, so can you."

Then there had been the pain of divorce and the dread of living in the same community with former spouses—the fear of step-siblings not getting along. I was still dealing with those problems, but we were adjusting.

I would make it through this ordeal too, I thought, and I gradually adjusted to the bumpy ride. It was going to be a long trip so I decided to enjoy it.

Soon it was time to stop for gas. We pulled into a roadside service station, and I prepared to take notes for my book. After all, that's what I'd come for—to interview people and to write about them.

The gas station

"My car broke down two years ago and I'm still here," explained the service attendant when I asked him what he was doing on the Alaska Highway. Several years before, he had nursed his antique jeep 3,000 miles up from California and was now pumping gas along the highway in British Columbia.

He checked our oil and tires and filled the tanks on both sides of our pickup as we chatted.

"Sixty-four cents a liter?" I gasped. "That's $2.50 a gallon!"

"Freight," he nodded. "Everything costs more up here because it has to be trucked in."

We paid 94 Canadian dollars to top off the tanks.

The attendant's wife, a slim girl with straight black hair and wearing a long gray sweat shirt, lounged inside the station behind the candy and snack counter devouring a Gothic romance. Besides the gas and oil, the California couple sold to tourists—at freight-inflated prices—such travel necessities as potato chips, canned pop, cheese, crackers and paperback books. I wondered whether she had read them all.

"How's business?" I asked her—trying to make conversation.

Parts of the Alaska Highway can be dusty and dangerous, but the scenery is incomparable.

"When you're 50 miles from any other gas station, you'll always have customers," she said, her eyes never leaving the book.

I felt properly put down and ambled back to the truck to jot down notes about the informal interior of the place and to bring my journal up-to-date. I also made a mental note to avoid acting like a typical tourist and not to ask such naive questions.

We told people that we were gathering material for a book. We had joked to our friends that we might look for jobs in Alaska. Our children worried that we might telephone home and say, "Pack your things, we're moving North." In reality, like thousands of gold rush stampeders whose spirits forever stalk the trails and streams of the Yukon, we were searching to find ourselves—or to find contentment.

With the pain of recent divorces still at the edge of our consciousness, Dave and I were beginning our odyssey. This trip, like our married life, was going to be a joint adventure—an experience shared. Or was it to be a joint adventure? Dave kept talking about hiking the 33-mile Chilkoot Trail. He seemed obsessed with his plan to backpack over the steep pass from Alaska into Canada following the route taken by gold miners in 1898. Meanwhile he was photographing some scenery and wildflowers and planned to put together a multimedia presentation for showing to friends who would be asking us about our impressions of Alaska.

We'd left our family in the lower 48 and prepared to drive the infamous Alcan. That was enough adventure for me. I didn't need a four-day hike on the Chilcoot trail. I'd seen photos of men trudging up that steep, snowy mountainside with enormous packs on their backs. Eventually we'd be deciding what to do about the Chilcoot, but first we had to get to Skagway.

We'd been warned the Alaska Highway would be rough, and we were physically prepared for the expected ordeal. Our new Ford 3/4-ton pickup truck, nicknamed Brown Bear by

Dave's daughter, Laura, was equipped with an auxiliary fuel tank, extra heavy duty tires and a CB radio. In addition, one of our last purchases before leaving home had been a screen that wrapped around the front of the truck to catch bugs and fend off flying stones.

With our gear—sleeping bags, firewood, cooking utensils, typewriter, cameras and clothing—stashed in the back, we were on our way. The truck was our transportation. An aluminum cap over the bed of the truck served as our rain-proof, bearproof, ready-pitched tent. At night we moved our luggage into the truck cab and rolled out our sleeping bags over a foam mattress in the back. A cooler, which could be plugged into the dashboard, rode on the seat between us much of the way. Dried fruits, staple foods, raincoats and boots helped fill up the back.

On a future trip we would travel and sleep more luxuriously in a Volkswagen Vanagon Camper, but on this first journey we were strictly roughing it.

Dave did most of the driving. I hated handling the truck. It was too big. But I loved being the navigator. On my lap was a copy of *The Milepost*, advertised as "the only All-the-North Travel Guide for Alaska, Yukon Territory, British Columbia, Northwest Territories and Alberta." Thick as the telephone directory of a medium-sized city, *The Milepost* contains mile-by-mile logs of all highways in Alaska and major travel routes through Western Canada. In addition, it contains specific information on towns, cities, parks, scenic attracions, customs requirements, time zones, airfields, ferry, airline, cruise and railroad schedules. Suggestions of where to go camping, fishing, hiking and rock hounding, see wildlife and wildflowers, have a picnic and view the pipeline were all contained between the covers.

In my opinion no one should travel to Alaska without a copy of the most recent edition of *The Milepost.* It was to be our handbook throughout the summer ahead.

Dave and I had been married only two years, having merged five teenagers into our "new family."The trauma and stress were beginning to wear off and we hoped the arrangement would work out. Now we were taking the summer to explore our feelings—interviewing whoever would talk to us and attempting to find out why other people seek new frontiers and wondering whether we should do the same.

We had dropped off my two daughters, sixteen-year-old-Marcia and fourteen-year-old Jodi, with my sister, Barbara, in Seattle. Laura, Dave's nineteen-year-old daughter, was on her own for the summer. My son Bruce and Dave's son Steve, both seventeen, were with their other parents.

Feeling a need ourselves to consider relocating or establishing new roots, we hoped to improve our insight by talking with others who had pulled up roots and started over. "What brought you North?" we planned to ask. "Did you discover what you were seeking? Did you escape what you were running away from? Are you happy?" We soon learned that those are the questions tourists ask the inhabitants of Alaska—if indeed they ask any questions. We would have to learn to be more subtle.

We were well aware that enterprising individuals have relocated everywhere. We could find such folks in our hometown of Kalamazoo, Michigan; but we thought we would probably find more people in Alaska with more 'extreme' stories.

Besides, I wanted to visit Alaska. I'd always thought someday I'd go there. I had long ago learned that this state was not full of Eskimos living in igloos—although my recollections from elementary school geography would have led me to believe that the entire region was covered with ice and snow the year around and that all residents hunted walrus and whales and herded reindeer.

The best bowl of chili

A tank full of gas further up the highway we pulled off at a place euphemistically called Steamboat Mountain Lodge.

"This diner with a gas pump looks like a dump," Dave said. But according to *The Milepost,* it was our only choice for miles.

"But look at the view!" I exclaimed.

It was beautiful. Steamboat Mountain Lodge boasts neither steamboat, nor mountain nor lodge; but from this remote, rickety, roadside restaurant there was a panoramic view of the distant Rockies. Somebody years ago thought that one of the ridges resembled the outline of a steamboat; hence the name.

The rustic, rugged roadhouse had a quaint charm of its own. Besides the two gas pumps and half a dozen primitive cabins, the "lodge" consisted of ten bar stools arranged in L-shape facing the counter in a long room the size of the vestibule of an average restaurant.

A slim, dark haired woman in her mid-20's greeted us; a toddler stuck his head in the door and a baby wearing only a diaper crawled at her mother's feet. This woman must be Sherilee Richter, we decided, for *The Milepost* mentioned that the establishment was owned by Sherilee and Robb Richter.

We were pleasantly surprised by the food. Sherilee advertised: "The best bowl of chili you've ever tasted." And she was right. It *was* the best chili and by the time we'd finished eating, we'd forgotten it was costing us $3.75 a bowl.

"I make up a big batch of chili—enough to serve 30 people—and freeze it so there's no waste," Sherilee explained to us as we ate. She also served apple pie that looked and tasted like the kind my grandmother used to bake. "But what are you doing here on the Alcan?" I asked her.

Ironically, some individuals seeking solitude, such as Sherilee and Robb, inadvertently put themselves into a business which becomes a hub of activity. At an impulsive moment several years before, the young Colorado couple had purchased the gas station and restaurant with living quarters attached. Steamboat Mountain Lodge, located about 350 miles from Dawson City, provided the only services along the rugged 90-mile stretch between Fort Nelson and Summit Lake.

License plates from throughout the United States and Canada decorate the yard outside Steamboat Mountain Lodge.

"Try and count our dollar bill wallpaper," urged Sherilee, changing the subject. The wall behind the counter in the restaurant was plastered with paper money from all over the world autographed by travelers through the years.

"If you tape up some currency, you're protected from inflation," the proprietress explained. "Whenever you return to the lodge, you can order anything from our menu at the same price it was when you were here before."

That offer might not last much longer, because Sherilee

and Robb were getting restless.

"We want to sell this place," Sherilee confided. "This isn't any place to raise kids." She scooped the baby up off the floor, stepped into the back room, changed the baby's diaper and returned with the toddler following her.

Sherilee said she hoped that by the time the children were school age they'd be living some place where school was more accessible. Perhaps they'd move to Fort Nelson or Whitehorse—or even Anchorage. She admitted the correspondence schools have a good reputation but said she and her husband hoped to have more social contacts for their children. I could understand that. I wouldn't want to raise a family miles and miles from anyone else, I thought. In addition to wanting a school, the couple sensed a need to live where there's a library and some place to put down roots.

Meanwhile, Steamboat Mountain had filled a gap for the Richters. It had satisfied their needs at one stage in their lives.

The place was for sale. Dave said, "Let's make an offer." My first thought was, "You're kidding. Who'd want to live in this godforsaken place? I couldn't see what owning and operating such a place as Steamboat Mountain Lodge would do for us.

But then I got to thinking—the phone wouldn't ring. I would have no more volunteer responsibilities. Oh, we couldn't buy such a place right now, of course. We still had children in high school. It would never do, I reasoned, to bring them to this kind of "No Man's Land." And I wouldn't want to give up the house we had just had built out in the country near Kalamazoo. But the idea did have some appeal. I thought I'd just like to experience living like this for a little while.

But no neighbors? No support system? I don't think I could take it for very long. But there would be lots of people coming and going. Would that be enough socialization? I was torn between craving the adventure and needing the security of friends and roots. I decided to table any such decision.

Skagway

In Skagway, the celebrated city that was the setting for Edna Ferber's novel, *Ice Palace,* we met the scrimshaw artist. Wearing a wool stocking cap, David Present was eating an ice cream cone while people swarmed about his handiwork spread out on several tables placed on the boardwalk in front of one of the shops.

He explained that the walrus ivory he carved was thousands of years old. It was beautiful, but since this was the first scrimshaw I'd seen, I had no way to judge its quality and value. Many scrimshaw artists' carvings picture Eskimos, dogs or wildlife. Present's intricate relief carvings, on the other hand, are often abstract and much more sophisticated. Many seem to have a life of their own.

"I use only fossilized walrus ivory," the artist explained. "—no fresh material. No animals are being killed for these sculptures." We learned that strict laws limit the taking and possession of walrus tusks to a few Alaskan native carvers.

Later we were to see other scrimshaw and to purchase a number of pieces for friends and family, but at that point we weren't ready to buy anything. A scrimshaw necklace I later bought for my sister Barbara, who lives in Seattle, has been

a favorite of hers, but my admiration for Present's work grew as I saw pieces of scrimshaw less skillfully carved by other artists around the state.

The street corner artist added local color to the scene in Skagway, and we could see that he was enjoying himself and perhaps making a living off his craft. But we were surprised to discover how well he had done. Five years later Present was the

David Present has found a good market in Skagway for his creativity.

proprietor of one of the most impressive galleries in Alaska. I arranged an interview to hear his success story.

David Present told us that he had grown up in Rochester, New York, majored in art and business at a school in Iowa, but couldn't see himself in business so he taught art and education in Iowa.

"I enjoyed teaching," David said, "but I felt a teacher must *do* what he teaches, so I took a year off and have never gone back to formal teaching. I moved from Iowa to Seattle, then jumped on a ferry and came to Skagway for what I thought would be a week. I fell in love with the town, and in three weeks had purchased a building for a shop.

"Immediately I began selling scrimshaw from a board laid across sawhorses in front of the building. As I collected money, I handed it back to the carpenter who had devised a moveable wall which we kept pushing back as another area of the shop was completed.

"Three years later I purchased another building so we could expand," he said.

Present and his wife Betsy helped each other through school and now Betsy is manager and buyer for the David Present Gallery which, besides showing David's increasingly impressive sculpture, features fifteen other artists.

"I insist that each artist receive 50% of the selling price because I'm in a position where I see the picture both from the artist's and the gallery owner's point of view," David said.

David conceives and designs many of his original pieces in Seattle during the winter and then spends summers sculpting in his Skagway studio.

"Marketing interferes with creativity," David said. "I never price a piece until it's in the gallery. I like to explore beautiful material. Once the image is in my mind, I can't create it fast enough."

David's pieces were sensuous and beautiful. They cried out to be touched and held, and I would have liked to purchase one but our discretionary budget didn't allow for accumulating expensive objects. Even the most beautiful works of art had to take second place to travel expenses. Everyone must make choices. We were no exception.

I hoped, however, that many other travelers would choose to buy David Present's work so he would be able to continue to spend his summers in Skagway.

Skagway's winter population of 300 or so hardy souls triples every summer as businesses along the boardwalk reopen to serve tourists arriving daily on ferries and cruise ships. At least that's how it was before the railroad shut down.

In past summers travelers would debark from ships that docked in Skagway, spend a few hours in the village and then board the White Pass and Yukon Railway. Some travelers would take the scenic ride all the way to Whitehorse. Others would go only as far as Lake Bennett where northbound and southbound trains met. They'd enjoy a traditional gold miner's lunch of baked beans, potato salad, homemade pie and coffee served in the Bennett station house and return the same day to Skagway.

The railroad closed in 1982 and since, the population of Skagway has diminished. However, residents of the village have become aware of the importance of tourism and there's a big push now to recapture the authentic gold rush appearance of the village. The National Park Service owns fourteen buildings and is renovating them as funds become available.

We watched as chattering tourists disembarked from an enormous white luxury liner. Skagway was the site where in 1897-98 gold seekers from San Francisco and Seattle unloaded their hastily assembled cargoes of scraggly horses, bales of hay, stacks of food, blankets, stoves, sleds, shovels and collapsible boats onto the dock. Then, miners' boots clomped along the boardwalks to the bars, beds and gambling tables of the Red Onion Saloon and the Golden North Hotel.

Today, as in the few brief months of Skagway's boom, boat passengers hurried with their money across weathered boardwalks into the shelter of some of these same establishments.

Dave and I found a room in an old Victorian style hotel which advertised rooms with a share-the-bath. Some of the young tourists shook their heads when they saw the accommodations, but we were delighted. This was something right out of a historical novel, and we loved it as we imagined ourselves a couple out of the past coming to Skagway to set up a business.

As we meandered around the village, Dave remarked, "We could open a photography shop here. I wonder if we'd get enough business from tourists to make it go?"

"How about a restaurant?" I suggested.

I soon thought better of this, however, because although I'd worked four summers as a waitress many years ago, the idea of being responsible for the cooking or for finding someone else to cook and wash dishes, day after day, exhausted me.

Since we know more about photography than about running a restaurant, we decided the photo shop would be the most appropriate for us. Or why not teach school here? Dave

Enterprising musher offers snowless dog sled rides in Skagway in June.

had been a college professor for seventeen years and I'd taught eight years before beginning a family. I'd always envied those courageous young women schoolteachers who went West on a stagecoach or train determined to bring education to the frontier.

Skagway is still, in some ways, a frontier. Today, however, the false-fronted wooden buildings, now converted into gift shops and restaurants, bring *gold* to the pockets of their canny proprietors without the backbreaking toil of digging deep into the frozen soil or panning nuggets from stream beds.

We enjoyed chatting with Skagway shopkeepers. One of them said that a boat had just arrived with fresh halibut, so we soon set out for a restaurant where we ordered steaks which had been cut from the tender, flaky white fish broiled in butter and served with lemon, a sprig of parsley and a baked potato. It was the best meal we'd eaten since leaving Seattle and we decided we'd enjoy Alaskan seafood whenever we had a choice.

Meanwhile, we continued to seek out historical sites we'd read about. With the reliable *Milepost* as our guide, we found Goldrush Graveyard only a mile and a half from downtown. Overgrown with weeds, the cemetery contains the weather-beaten graves of local lawman Frank Reid and *town boss* Soapy Smith.

We had watched a cast of live actors perform "The Soapy Smith Show" and "Skagway in the Days of '98" at a storefront theater. The Soapy Smith Show gives a detailed account of the life and times of the charismatic con man who ruled Skagway from August 1897 until the gunfight in July 1898 against Frank Reid that took the lives of both men.

At the cemetery we brushed aside grass and vines to decipher names and dates on long-neglected grave markers of miners and early settlers. Many of the wooden crosses tilted precariously. Others had already fallen.

Near the graveyard, we took a short hike to Reid Falls. Tramping along the lush green trail, we tried to picture ourselves living here some eighty years ago. We soon decided the novelty would probably not have lasted very long.

The following day as we continued to explore the area in our pickup, we followed a bumpy dirt road that snaked along the inlet from Skagway to the remains of the short-lived town of Dyea. Here in the winter of 1898, thousands of gold seekers began the tortuous 33-mile hike through a 3,739 foot high notch in the mountains known as Chilkoot Pass.

For many stampeders, the Chilkoot Trail was the gateway to the gold fields—the overland portion of a four hundred mile journey across a chain of Canadian lakes and down the Yukon River to legendary Dawson City. For years it had been Dave's dream to hike that trail. I was satisfied to sample the beginning of the Chilkoot Trail which we did before driving back to Skagway.

Skagway was really our introduction to Alaska and although it wasn't a typical town—too many tourists—it whetted our appetite. We determined to see as much of the 49th state as we had time to cover in the remaining six weeks we had set aside for our first journey North.

Already I was beginning to feel the way I usually feel whenever I visit a place to which I'm attracted. I want to explore every corner. I don't want to leave it. I don't like skimming the surface. To me, a tourist who asks, "How long does it take to *do* Skagway?" is missing half the fun. I couldn't stand to be on a canned tour where tourists stop to take photos and then jump back on the bus.

In our attempt to live our trip and not just photograph it, we took even fewer photos than we ordinarily would have taken. When time is limited, we've found it's almost impossible both to see something and to photograph it.

We could stop whenever and wherever we wanted to. But if we dallied, we'd see very little of Alaska. At the end of our third day, we knew it was time to move on. Reluctantly we said good-bye to Skagway, but only with the promise to ourselves that we would return.

Bed and breakfast in Skagway

Five years later we did return to Skagway. We found the Skagway Inn was under new management. An attractive brunette with long curls and wearing a black dress from the gay nineties era greeted us and took our reservations for the following evening. She was already booked up for that night so we decided to sleep in our van as we had done en route. On this trip we had driven our new cream colored Volkswagon Vanagon Camper with a pop-up top so we could stand up inside. The van rode much more comfortably than Brown Bear and had a tiny sink, stove and refrigerator as well as cupboard space and a comfortable bed. The best thing was being able to set up camp on a rainy evening without having to rearrange our gear or leave the vehicle.

Suzanne Mullen had recently become part owner of the Skagway Inn. She was acting manager and was remodeling the inn, making it into the town's only official Bed and Breakfast establishment. She seemed very professional and made a note of when we'd be back. Then she said we could use the showers that day since her overnight guests weren't checking in until much later that evening.

I was to stay at the inn the two following nights while Dave hiked the Chilkoot Trail. Yes, Dave had determined that on this trip he was going the length of the trail and doing it alone. I sensed that he really didn't think I would be able to keep up with him so I was to remain in Skagway. After all, his strides are about two to one of mine. I began to feel the way the miners' wives must have felt even though Dave's trip was to take only three days.

If I were to go, it would take five or six days, Dave had told me. Besides he'd have to carry a heavier pack—twice as much food and water, a larger tent, two sleeping bags and a change of clothing. Of course I could carry some, but he didn't think

David Present carves with antique ivory.

Suzanne Mullen, proprietor of the Skagway Inn, offers tours of the town as well as bed and breakfast.

I could carry as much as he could. Probably not. I'm 5' 5". He's 6 feet tall and has had much more practice than I have carrying heavy loads. Besides he had purchased a new backpack for himself. None for me. It was pretty obvious that he wanted to go alone. He wanted to do something macho himself and not have a woman tagging along. He never exactly said that, but his "You'll have a better time staying in Skagway," wasn't very subtle.

I looked around the inn and noticed the names of the rooms. They were the same as they were at the turn of the century. All of the rooms bore names of ladies of the evening such as Irene,

Mabel and Opal who entertained miners. Many of the furnishings were from the gold rush era also; but modern plumbing and respectable clientele have improved the inn's reputation.

For breakfast Suzanne set out fruit, cinnamon rolls, muffins, small boxes of cereal and left a note: "Help yourself to milk in the refrigerator."

The milk came from Seattle in small rectangular boxes. The fine print on the side claimed a shelf life of more than six months. Of course, milk tastes best when cold and Suzanne had an ample supply chilling for her house guests.

Suzanne intrigued me and I wanted to know what brought her to Skagway. I learned that she had been married nine years, was divorced and started back to school at the University of Colorado.

"But I soon decided that going back to school wasn't what I wanted," she said. (Her two young sons were living with their father in another state at that time.)

"I met someone who was headed for Alaska; and I decided I'd like to ride along with him," Suzanne said. "I asked him if he could wait two days while I got ready to go. He did and we were off. This fellow kept telling me that his brother and I would get along well together. I arrived in Alaska and met his brother. We did get along well and lived together in the bush for three years in a cabin on the Yukon River northeast of Fairbanks.

"That was a good experience," Suzanne recalled. "I developed strength those years in the cabin. I survived—sometimes by luck and other times by sheer determination."

I envied Suzanne her independence and courage and when I told her that, she said, "I suppose I look like a strong and independent woman, but sometimes I go sit down and cry because I'm so scared—of what the future may bring.

"Some things are more difficult in Alaska," she said. "Others are easier. Here one can be a big fish in a little pond. There are opportunities and you're not limited just because you're a woman. They don't grade you on sex or education.

They grade you on what you can do.

"But you have to grab what you want," she added. "You can't sit and wait for things to happen.

"After living in the bush three years, I'd depleted my savings. So I began working in a restaurant in Fairbanks where I earned up to $500 a week in tips. Then during the oil boom in 1975 and '76, I washed dishes in Prudhoe Bay for a salary of $1,000 a week."

The bonanaza ended after the pipeline was completed. When she and hundreds of others lost their jobs on the North Slope, Suzanne came to Skagway, bought a 15-passenger van and offered tours to vacationers arriving on the cruise ships.

To attract guests to her tours, Suzanne offers salmon quiche and historical information. She has researched the area and tells tourists interesting stories about the history of Skagway, Dyea and surrounding places.

"For instance, one time the bank here in Skagway was robbed; and nobody was hurt except the robber," Suzanne said. "He took a stick of dynamite with him when he went to rob the bank. Somehow the dynamite exploded and blew his head off. They buried his head and body in different places. What a humiliation for the robber."

That's just one of many stories Suzanne tells the folks who sign up for her personalized small group tours.

Suzanne had been spending winters in Juneau, sometimes working in a legislator's office. This would be her first winter in Skagway for she was committed to keeping the bed and breakfast open year-round. She figured that since the new road from Skagway to Whitehorse would be open in the winter this year for the first time that would bring in extra business.

Mother Confessor

Some women, like Suzanne, go to Alaska to get away from

their husbands. Others, like Marge Newell, come with their husbands. Marge arrived in Skagway in 1978 as a minister's wife. The night after Dave had taken off on the Chilkoot Trail, I wanted something to do besides work on my book, so I was happy when Suzanne suggested we meet Marge at the Red Onion Saloon.

Over cokes and beer, Marge said, "My husband Ken had always wanted to live in Alaska. I told him, 'Go right ahead.' I didn't believe I could survive in a native village. We had a son still in school. But when someone suggested that we look at Skagway, we did and we loved it.

"We found an old church building and a dead congregation. There were three of us in church that first Sunday, but we began to maintain and restore that old building and we became a part of things. As it turned out, our ministry in the community extended far beyond the church itself."

Marge said that she played the first summer and then went to work at the Klondike Hotel as a night auditor but found she didn't like corporate life. She tried subbing in the local school system but found she wasn't born to teach either. So she purchased a small gift shop.

When her husband retired from the ministry and returned to the Lower 48, Marge went with him. But she returned this summer to run the gift shop.

"I suppose I'm trying to sell the business," she said. "I need to be done with it."

But somehow she didn't seem in a hurry to leave the village. I wasn't eager to leave it either. I'd been here only a few days and it was beginning to feel like home.

I could identify with Marge's struggle to find her niche. Yet as she talked I kept thinking—"I wish I could stay here and try these things. I could work in a restaurant or a hotel. I could teach. I could manage a store. Oh, to just be here and become part of the community. I don't like being a visitor or a tourist."

Now, eight years later, Marge has become a fixture in Skagway. But even more—she is sort of Mother Confessor to local residents. College kids who come up to work for the summer check in with her regularly and use her home as a meeting place, a place to have their mail forwarded and a place to receive phone calls from home. They tell Marge their troubles, often ask her advice and sometimes take it. Marge had found her forte.

The next day I talked to Bob Dietrick who was clerking in a jewelry store in Skagway.

"It was fun living on the East coast," Bob said. "I could jump in my car and drive to the beach. Alaska was a complete change for me, but I'll never be sorry I moved up here.

"I was working in a grocery store Outside and doing substitute teaching. (Alaskans refer to anywhere besides Alaska as Outside). I applied for a teaching position in Alaska and almost immediately the superintendent of schools in Skagway called and asked me three questions: '1) Are you certified? 2) How much experience have you had? and 3) How soon can you get here?' I was hired on the telephone.

"I flew into Juneau and then took the ferry on up to Skagway. The wind was blowing. It was raining when I arrived—very yucky weather—and there was nobody to meet me. Finally, a friendly travel agent drove me through a number of potholes to the school where I was greeted by secretaries in pigtails and bobby socks. Then along came the superintendent wearing a 1940's suit. What a cultural shock until I realized it was 50's day at school.

"Next, I found there were no apartments in Skagway. I bounced around town in a truck and was ready to leave. But I got involved with the community, the library and other activities and decided to stay. Back home in the Lower 48 I was one of many. Here I'm one of a few. What makes it special is that the year-round residents are like an extended family."

Bob explained that after living five years in Skagway, he accepted a job in Juneau where he had taught for the past six years but he still spends his summers working in Skagway.

Another interview that I tackled while Dave was gone was Sean Lyon, David Present's apprentice. Sean was from our home town of Kalamazoo, Michigan. Wearing black jeans, striped shirt and sandals, 27-year-old Sean sat in the shop behind the David Present Gallery polishing an antique ivory walrus tusk. Using tools similar to those of a dentist, Sean creates small pieces of his own from fossilized ivory and helps

Sean Lyon says he finds ivory carving relaxing.

Present polish larger pieces.

"Some of this ivory is from mammoths, found in old river beds," he said. "It may be anywhere from 5,000 to 100,000 years old. These tusks were discarded in garbage piles centuries ago. The Inuit Eskimos now are digging 20 to 30 feet down into the frozen tundra, finding ivory and selling it.

"Ivory carving is helping me to pay back my college loans," Sean said. "It was at Western Michigan University in Kalamazoo that I became interested in sculpture."

Sean also was working half time as a mental health counselor in Skagway. He found that by having two part time jobs, he not only could earn his keep and help pay his college loans, but also find variety for himself. Burnout occurs easily among people working in the counseling field, so the carving provided a change of pace for him.

"Carving and working here in the ivory shop help me keep my sanity," he said.

The next day I packed a lunch and prepared to hike by myself on one of the less demanding trails just outside of Skagway. The rangers at the Park Service visitors' center provided a map, but the most difficult part was finding exactly where in town to catch the beginning of the trail. After a couple of false starts, I was on my way. The trail was fairly rugged but of course nothing like the Chilkoot. I felt quite independent as I made my way along the path. At occasional lookout points, I stopped and rested and thought about Dave on The Chilkoot.

I was having a bit of difficulty following the ranger's map. When another hiker on the trail, whom I kept running into as we tried following the maps, suggested we hike together, I agreed it made sense. We settled on a trail that looked feasible and continued, closely following the map.

At noon, we pooled our sack lunches at a table we discovered. Larry, my new companion from Texas, was taking a cruise with his parents and two sons. His wife had died several months earlier so this was sort of a passage time in his life. He, too, was trying to sort things out. We chatted about our children and exchanged small talk as we scanned the views from the mountainside. We exchanged addresses and phone numbers when we returned to Skagway and he promised to send me his recipe for gaspacho soup.

The Klondike show

That evening I decided to take in the floor show in the Klondike Hotel Lounge. Although I didn't relish the thought of attending alone, there weren't many alternatives. I could stay in the inn and read and write. Or I could call Larry on the cruise ship and see if he would show me around the ship.

Larry said he was having trouble finding people to dance with him and he had said his ship wasn't scheduled to leave the dock until the next morning. I really would like to have seen the ship. If he were patient, I could dance.

I decided against any of these options—even though I was a bit disgusted at Dave for taking off on the Chilkoot Trail without me. I decided I could go gather more material at the Klondike by myself. I went to the show and was delighted to find that it was more of an audience participation program than a night club act.

Singing "Tulips from Amsterdam," Gillian Campbell marched into the lounge wearing a black and white outfit with white flowers on her large hat and sporting long black eyelashes and long curls. Gillian, known as the "Belle of the Yukon," was ready for the audience and they responded. The lounge was crowded with middle-aged couples who had plunked down $5 apiece for the show which featured songs from the Gay '90s.

Accompanied by piano player Darrel Steinger, who swept his fingers across the honky-tonk ivories with ease, Gillian tugged at the heart strings and funny bones of the audience. As

Gillian sang, "I'm Going to File My Claim," she ruffled the hair of one of the gentlemen in the audience. He loved it. Later she asked for a volunteer and proceeded to sit on his lap while she sang another number.

I felt at home when Gillian had the crowd link hands and sing, "Casey would waltz with a strawberry blonde and the band played on..." and "Daisy, Daisy, give me your answer true..." And when it came time for the song, "Makin' Whoopie," we all chimed in at the proper signal. At other times, we clapped or sang particular parts. With the aid of song sheets supplied by Gillian, we sang along with many of the sixty-two numbers listed on the sheet.

The piano player had grown up in Saskatchewan, Canada. "I'm twenty years behind my time," he said and gave impersonations of Al Jolson, Jimmy Durante and other popular entertainers from the past.

Later, balloons were handed out. We in the audience blew them up, tied them and then pushed them to the ceiling as we sang, "I'm Forever Blowing Bubbles."

Gillian had provided a nostalgic trip into the past. I'd had a good time even though I'd gone by myself. I walked back to the Skagway Inn, typed a few notes with my portable typewriter and called it a day.

By the time I was to pick up Dave with the van, I was exhaused from nervous anticipation. Dave and I had driven the 27 miles together to a place called Log Cabin a few days before he left so I would know the route. But I knew it all too well. Along Klondike Highway 2 as it crosses into Canada is some of the most beautiful scenery in North America, but the newly paved road twists and winds and the gorges, canyons and drop-offs gave me a queasy stomach.

I thought if I had company it would give me courage to make the drive, so I invited three women who were also staying at the Skagway Inn to come along. They were sisters, traveling together on a once-in-a-lifetime trip to Alaska. I'd been talking with them the night before and when I asked if they wanted to ride with me through White Pass into Canada, they accepted my offer immediately. If my driving scared them, they didn't mention it , and we made it to the designated parking lot without incident.

The spot on the map called Log Cabin is the place where the Klondike Highway intersects with the abandoned railroad. No buildings remain, but the site was a gold rush town in 1898. I parked the van and we got out and looked around. I started walking down the railroad tracks where we expected to meet Dave.

Where was he? Should I have gone with him? What if he

Dave Curl returns from hiking the Chilcoot Trail.

had fallen off a cliff? There may have been more snow than he had expected. What if he had collapsed from exhaustion? Had he taken enough food and water? Where was he?

After twenty minutes of walking, we spied a figure in the distance. It was Dave. Never had I been so relieved to see him.

He looked tired but seemed bouyed up by the excitment of his accomplishment.

Dave was very thirsty so we hurried back to the van. His water bottles were empty because he had underestimated how long it would take to walk back along the tracks to Log Cabin, but luckily in the van we had a can of Vernors ginger ale I had brought from Michigan. This relieved his thirst, and we headed back to Skagway where he spent the rest of the day drying out his wet clothes and tent—and resting.

Later, Dave really began talking about the trip. It had been even more rugged than he had imagined, but he had always felt in control—even when he was nearly waist deep in the snow. If he had been scared, he wasn't about to admit it.

"I passed from summer to fall to winter to spring on the three day hike," he explained. "The trail went literally from season to season." I envied him the accomplishment and the experience, but somehow I thought it was important that he had done it and done it alone. Besides I'm not sure how I would have handled snow up to my armpits. I believed I would have managed, somehow, because when survival is at stake, most of us can make it. But I was glad he had done his thing, alone—the way he wanted to do it.

Eagle

Several days later it was still raining and I was cold. The night before, after a white-knuckle drive over the "Top of the World" Highway from Dawson City, Dave and I had huddled in a campground called Liberty. Along this narrow, gravel road, westward from Dawson City in the Yukon into Alaska, we had driven past some of the most beautiful scenery in the world, but I hadn't been able to enjoy it. It was just too scary.

"If you're taking any more of these side trips, I'm going to Anchorage and stay there," I told Dave. "I'm not going on any more dangerous roads, holding my breath—wondering if the next curve will be the last and dreading that we might go plummeting over a cliff."

I'd wondered, feared—how it would be if we went over. Would we be jounced down with our supplies all scattered, but with us unharmed? Or would we end up injured or killed with no one knowing we were even there until weeks later when they found our bodies. We'd already discovered that the CB radio we had purchased especially for this trip was useless. We'd not been able to contact anyone during trial attempts on the highway. The mountains blocked transmissions, and seldom was anyone within range anyway.

Our visit to Skagway had been a good experience; the town is a living museum—a tourist attraction—a place everyone who travels to Alaska should visit because it gives one a sense of the history of the 49th state. But we reminded each other that we had come to Alaska to learn about people who are living here now—to learn what compelled them to leave their former places of residence—what brought them to the place many call America's last frontier.

Now we were nearing Eagle without mishaps—anticipating our first real experience in a 'bush' Alaskan community. We had chosen Eagle because it was at the end of a road and because we'd been intrigued by tales we'd read about this rustic village alongside the Yukon River.

Friday morning when we arrived in the sleeping little town of rough log and frame houses, our watches showed 9 a. m. "Where is everyone?" I asked. Not a soul was stirring. Eagle was like a ghost town.

Of course it had long been daylight. Since it was the third of July, the sun really never set. It now seemed to us as if it were the middle of the day.

We drove up one narrow street and down another. The cabins were shuttered. Even the dogs were silent. Parked in front of one cabin was the pickup and trailer—with California license plates—that had so impatiently passed us during the night on the gravel road leading from the Top of the World Highway northward on the Taylor Highway to Eagle.

When the driver had sped around us, gravel flying up from his tires, we had assumed correctly that he was headed for the same destination we were; at this point Eagle is the only place you can go on the Taylor Highway.

Now our competitor for the road was sleeping with his possessions still lashed to the trailer while we drove up and down the deserted streets.

Once we were in Eagle, there were only two ways to

drive—back the way we had come, or along the road running roughly parallel with the Yukon River. The river road begins in the school grounds at the Indian village three miles east and terminates at the airstrip on the other side of town.

Finally we parked Brown Bear, got out and started walking. The rain had let up and it felt good to stretch our legs. As we walked around Eagle, we noted a strange contrast between the apparent lack of materialism and the enthusiasm for civic activity. "Keep America Reading," was a motto posted on the book drop in front of a new one room log cabin library, two doors from the post office.

A list of new books in the library was posted on the bulletin

Volunteers staff the Eagle library.

board inside the post office. Some of the books were: *Nulato Indian Life* by Carlo; *White Water* by Erskine; *Rodales' Guide to Compost, A Solar Greenhouse Book,* and *Building and Using Sun Heated Greenhouses.* There was also a book about recycling and another about teaching in Alaska.

The bulletin board outside the post office announced a trap

shoot, a salmon bake and a parade for the upcoming July 4th holiday weekend. One sign requested wide mouth jars for the carnival. We never did find out what the jars were used for, but I presumed they were wanted for a drop-the-clothespin contest or a similar game.

Eventually, people began stirring and we finally realized we had crossed two time zones during the night and what we'd thought was 9 a. m. was actually 7 a. m.

About 10 a. m., Eagle time, we met several students from a mission college in Bethel, a city in Western Alaska accessible only by plane or boat. The students had just arrived in Eagle ready to conduct a Bible School for the local children;

Eagle museum (right) was once the old Federal courthouse.

meanwhile, this morning they, like we, were interested in visiting the village museum in the old federal courthouse.

One of the students had borrowed a key from the sleepy curator and invited us to browse through the building with their group.

After touring the museum, we wandered over to the library. Staffed by volunteers, it is the cultural center of town, and although strangers, we were greeted warmly by the volunteer librarians for the day—a visiting anthropologist and his wife from Colorado. The couple told us they planned to spend the year in Eagle to study the effect isolation has on people. They explained that in winter, Eagle is completely shut off from the rest of the world except for the mail plane that attempts to land twice a week and the lone satellite-relay telephone in Helmer's general store.

The thought of isolation seemed both appealing and repelling to me. It would be nice to have a whole winter just to read, write, think and work crossword puzzles, I thought, and I could understand the importance of the library. I could be at home anywhere in a library.

I remembered how I used to frequent a library about seven miles from the farmhouse in Michigan that my first husband Paul and I had rented when the children were small. I'd go and load up on picture books for the children and historical novels for myself.

To have the whole winter to read without interruption would be terrific, I thought. But no driving from village to village? I like to travel as well as to read. Maybe Eagle would not be the place for me. But I wanted to see as much of the village as possible now that I was here.

Sarge and Fort Egbert

The dirt roads near Eagle were free of snow in July. From the library we explored as far as Fort Egbert, a turn-of-the-century U. S. Army post that is slowly being restored into another museum for the village.

A steady drizzle began, so we pulled on our lightweight windbreaker parkas which we had donned nearly every day since arriving in Alaska. We were seldom caught in a downpour that required our *real* raincoats, but we were always reaching for the 60/40 parkas.

Dave has been a photographer for more than 30 years; therefore, he found the photo display of the history of the fort especially interesting. After we had looked at the photos, we were given a tour of the stables, dog kennels, mule barn and officers' quarters by Jim Waller, who is known to everyone as Sarge.

We guessed Sarge to be about fifty years old. At this time he was mayor of Eagle as well as the caretaker and chief tour guide at the fort. His rumpled fatigue clothes seemed appropriate for the tour and his broad brimmed GI hat kept the rain off his head.

"It's all part of my job," he explained when we questioned whether he had time to show us around Fort Egbert that rainy morning. He said that the Park Service had restored the post—"as far as they had money to do it."

Sarge is also a volunteer fire fighter and an outfitter and guide for hunters and fishermen. Being an outfitter meant he would supply food, clothing, guns, fishing poles and lures, backpacks, sleeping bags, rain gear, boots—whatever the camper, hunter or fisherperson wanted. Many visitors brought with them more enthusiasm than experience so Sarge would provide the novices with both supplies and advice.

Sarge said, "I grew up in Massilon, Ohio and then I joined the Marines as soon as I could leave home, but I'd heard stories from a neighbor about the gold rush stampede and seen pictures of Alaska and furs from here when I was nine years old."

Twenty years ago when Sarge's enlistment expired, (after eleven years in the U. S. Marine Corps), he came to hunt and fish in Alaska and decided to stay. His wife Louise was village clerk in Eagle for a time; now she occupies herself making decorative knick knacks to sell to occasional tourists, like us, who wander into town.

One popular item pokes fun at Alaska's wildlife. Louise refers to these six-inch-long insects as 'moosequitoes' because they're manufactured from oval peanut-sized moose droppings, glued together, shellacked and painted.

The Wallers' ancient frame house, once painted white, serves as headquarters for Sarge's river guide business. On the weathered wooden clapboards outside their home located

Sarge Waller is mayor, caretaker, tour guide and outfitter for hunters and fishermen.

a few blocks from the center of town, hang—in typical frontier fashion—souvenirs including a couple of life preservers with Japanese inscriptions reminiscent of Sarge's days in the Marines.

Louise also does laundry for the miners as the village has no laundromat. "Louise has a big washer and dryer," Sarge explained. "There are very few household appliances of any kind in Eagle."

Another good reason not to spend a whole winter in Eagle, I thought. Still, the people were magnetic. I wanted to know them better. There was a genuineness about them—as if they cared about the really important things—like the largest American flag in town which waved proudly from a pole in front of the Wallers' house and laundry.

The Eagle's Nest

After spending a couple of hours reliving the old days with Sarge Waller, we were hungry and proceeded toward The Eagle's Nest, a restaurant whose ad in *The Milepost* had attracted our attention.

"Fresh pies and doughtnuts daily, hard ice cream, shakes, pizza," I'd read aloud to Dave as we had traveled along the highway the day before. Finally, at the square frame building that housed the restaurant, we weren't quite sure whether 'Outsiders' would be welcome or not. Posted outside the Eagle's Nest, as well as on some of the businesses and cabins in the village, were crudely lettered signs proclaiming such friendly slogans as "Government keep out." "Take your business elsewhere" and "Antiquities Act illegal. Period."

We soon learned that 1978 legislation had upset many Alaskan bushfolk when the federal government designated as national park land millions of acres where they had hunted and fished for years without regulation. Referred to as the Antiquities Act, what was perceived as government interference had hit particularly hard in Eagle. Three years later, people were still fuming at the legislation. Another sign on the door of the town's only hardware store proclaimed: "Park Service stay out."

Tensions were still running high and it seemed risky for anyone wearing a short haircut or a green uniform to set foot inside the town. Apparently, Dave's Air Force haircut was all that was needed to bring a burly bull of a backwoodsman charging over to stand belly to belly and confront him.

At six feet, Dave seldom has to look up to people, but this

fellow must have drawn himself up to 6' 6" as he glowered down past his scruffy beard.

"You aren't an agent from the park service, are you?" growled the big woodsman. His matted blond hair was tied in place with a band torn from his tattered denim jacket.

But his gruffness turned into a grin when we explained that we were writing a book and asked him whether he would like to be in it.

"Friends call me Bob," he said, extending his hand and explaining that he had come into the country seven years before, just after completing a degree in business management from a small college in Pennsylvania. The lure of a pipeline job was irresistible then and seems better to Bob today than any of the 9-5 routines engaged in by his college classmates. Bob hunts and fishes all summer and puts in long hours on pipeline maintenance in the winter when the fair weather workers flee back to Texas.

"I can earn $2,400 a week in the winter—working 13 hours a day," Bob said. "Ecologically I'm against what the pipeline is doing to land and wildlife and I would have fought it if I'd lived here ten years ago, but as long as it's already here and pays good money, I don't mind cashing their checks."

Bob also enjoys not being tied down by schedules or regulations. "I'll abide by the rules of the park service," he said shrugging his shoulders, "but I don't like anyone telling me when and where I can or cannot hunt, fish, trap or build a cabin."

We wondered whether Bob's attitude was typical, realized we were still hungry, and continued on our way to the Eagle's Nest.

The waitress was pleasant and the knotty pine interior, the red checkered tablecloths and the aroma of freshly brewed coffee made us feel welcome. Miners, teachers and fishermen sipped their morning coffee, and visitors had no other place to eat unless they wanted to cook their own meals.

This was no fast food restaurant, but the food was quickly

prepared to order. Yes, everything was homemade—literally—by the owner, and the French toast, eggs, hash browns and doughnuts all looked good. The hotcakes and eggs we ordered were delicious.

I like to eat breakfast out—anywhere, anytime—and this breakfast in Eagle has been a pleasant memory of our trip and of breakfast for all times. Dave has framed a placemat from the restaurant and it hangs on a wall with other Alaskan memories.

Yes, the food was expensive compared to restaurants in the lower 48, but the atmosphere compensated for the cost. Besides, it was raining again, and we hadn't felt like cooking breakfast over a campfire. We'd have plenty of opportunities to cook when we were on the road again.

The Eagle's Nest, like the library and post office, was a meeting place where people were ready and willing to talk. No one seemed to be going anywhere in particular and no one seemed to have anything pressing to do. Later, they'd be out dredging gold or fishing on the river, but while people were here in the restaurant, they relaxed.

At a table next to us sat Bill Walker with his wife and son. Walker wasted no words. He had come from Texas to Alaska to make money, he told us. And he had done it. He said he'd made his fortune mining coal and in his spare time likes to hunt and fish. His young wife sells real estate.

"The money is in the natural resources—gold, coal and oil," he said as he hauled out his fat wallet, peeled off a $100 bill and slapped it down to pay for his family's breakfast.

As we sat lazily finishing our tea, we decided the Eagle's Nest was both a symbol of a peaceful village where no one was in a hurry and also an example of people mining gold without having to dig or dredge for it.

But we soon learned that the restaurant had brought its owners neither peace nor profit. When the crowd thinned out, we approached the attractive young woman who attended both grill and counter. Her name was Linda Nelson.

"When my husband Jerry and I bought the Eagle's Nest, the place was pretty run down," Linda said. "We planned to fix up the building, get a good business going and then sell out at a profit."

So far, they'd found no buyer.

"Why not keep the restaurant?" we asked Linda as we eyed the For Sale sign in the window.

"Because I want to do nothing—like others around here," she answered. "I want to play with my kids—not work a grill night and day."

Linda's and Jerry's experience set me to thinking. Would Dave and I be self-directing enough to start our lives over again in Alaska? Could we build a new business and make it thrive or would we survive by continuing in freelance writing and photography?

I had been writing more than twelve years. By promising editors specific material by a definite date, I'd forced myself to meet deadlines and to produce. I'd learned that a firm deadline gets articles finished, but something speculative usually ends up in the "pending" file. Too many of my files were labeled "miscellaneous," as Dave pointed out one day when I was being particularly virtuous about how well organized I was.

Each of us has our own particular style, and I was already beginning to realize one's drive, self-discipline and work habits don't necessarily depend on geography. Right there in The Eagle's Nest I began to examine my own lifestyle more closely. Perhaps introspection would help me to undertand others' lifestyles better, too.

Helmers' general store

We headed back toward Helmers' store where potted geraniums bloom on the window sills and caribou antlers decorate the doorway. T-shirts imprinted "Eagle, Alaska—on the Yukon" in small, medium, large and extra large hang from the ceiling. Hiking boots, outdoor clothing and hand tools are crammed into bins in the back room. Canned goods and staples at frontier prices line crude shelves; cold pop and ice cream bars fill the refrigerator. A steady stream of people come in to use the telephone in the corner by the door. Why? Because it's the only phone in town.

"How do you dial long distance?" Dave asks the fellow behind the counter of the general store.

"Every call from here is long distance," responds Ralph Helmer, the proprietor.

The satellite telephone is one of the Helmers' more lucrative ventures. It's a monopoly, and, like shortwave radios, the phone is Eagle's direct link with the world outside. For a flat fee for each call plus the toll charge, one can call anywhere in the world. After getting the hang of push-to-talk phoning, we manage to ring up our children back in Michigan for about $3.00 a minute.

In Eagle the local kitchen-to-kitchen gossip line is the CB radio.

"Everybody in town monitors channel 21," we are told. Surprisingly, it seems that television has found its way to nearly every remote corner of the globe. Eagle, Alaska is no exception. Folks tend to gather in the cabins at villages that have subscribed. Even in Eagle villagers can watch *The Beverly Hillbillies, Mash,* or *Dallas* on the new satellite cable TV channel.

"We enjoy video cassette movies during the winter," explains one of the villagers. "We've no time for them during the summer."

Ralph and Sue Helmer dominated the business scene in Eagle by creating their own opportunities. The Helmers own a thriving grocery and general store and operate the town's only motel, electric utility and telephone company.

"Ralph is one of the few real hustlers in town," we were

told by one of the townspeople, with a wink and a trace of envy. An engineer for the gas utility in Anchorage, Ralph had come with Susie to Eagle six years earlier to get away from the city. They bought the grocery and motel from Postmaster John Borg and immediately brought in a diesel generator to provide enough electricity for their own planned enterprises and surplus power to sell other residents who wanted to wire into the system.

Thus Helmers' General Store is the home of the local electric company. Besides generating and selling electricity to a dozen village residents, they also rent out freezer space or floor space to set up a freezer. The next addition was going to

Helmers' General Store is hub of commerce in Eagle.

be a domestic laundry, we were told. Currently some of the residents use gasoline powered washing machines.

Ralph drives his 1 1/2 ton truck to Anchorage regularly to replenish stock for the store, but the largest loads are in the fall when he has to lay in a supply of "a lot of everything,"—enough to last most of the town folk and river people all winter.

"Can you imagine trying to figure out how much brown sugar, salt, canned soup and detergent the entire population of Eagle might need during the seven months that the village is 'snowed in?'." I asked Dave.

He shook his head and said, "I don't think I'd want to own a grocery here or anywhere." Again, however, we found ourselves imagining settling in Alaska and finding some way to earn a living.

So far no one had really encouraged us to move to Alaska, although people we met were friendly enough. It was as if those who had migrated to Alaska had come in and shut the door behind them. Some seemed to feel that the state would be too crowded if anyone else came to stay. Everyone wanted to be the last to settle on the last frontier.

It was raining still, so instead of spending another soggy night in our pick-up, we rented one of Helmers' rustic cabins. We dodged the rain, dashing across the road to the toilet and unheated shower rooms. The water was hot, however, and since we hadn't had a warm shower for a couple of days, we didn't mind jumping puddles to get one.

Susie and Ralph Helmer like Alaska and its challenges. They have good heads for business; they see needs and set out to meet them. They work hard and they enjoy it. Entrepreners like the Helmers would be successful anywhere, but they're outstanding in Eagle because there are plenty of opportunities and a shortage of competitors.

When we returned five years later, the Helmers had moved. But not far. They had sold the general store, but they still owned the electric utility and the telephone company. Some two or three dozen phone numbers were posted beside the town's only pay phone—in front of the variety store the Helmers now operate. Sue was behind the counter inside the store, but a 25% off sidewalk sale was going on outside.

Wanted: a middle-aged bride

On our first trip to Eagle, Ralph Helmer had suggested we might want to look up Harvey Black. Like countless former military people, Harvey Black came to Alaska for adventure. After being introduced to the Arctic by Uncle Sam, the 57 year-old retired Army master sergeant served his last tour of active duty as a recruiter in the Alaskan bush, helping the Army fill its quota of native American enlistees.

Sergeant Black also used the opportunity to establish connections useful to him now in the trading business which supplements his GI pension.

Wearing a Buffalo Bill Cody beard and sideburns, the sergeant still looks like a soldier—but from the old cavalry days. The front yard outside his cabin, like the yards of many of his neighbors, was crammed with "resources." A dog sled, several cords of firewood, a GMC diesel pickup, a Honda motorcycle, old radio equipment and an abandoned oil barrel stove occupied much of the yard. The rest seemed to be spare parts.

In the Arctic nothing is thrown away because it might be useful someday and everything costs so much to ship in. "It looks like a junkyard in July," someone said, "but remember, it's covered with snow most of the year."

The wooden frame home near the river road looked new and freshly painted. Harvey had built it for his most recent wife, who walked out of his solitary life even more abruptly than she had entered it. Harvey described his recent whirlwind courtship. "I met her on Halloween, married her on Valentine's Day, and she was gone by the 4th of July." We never learned why she left, but we could only surmise that she had been more attracted to the excitement of urban life.

"I'm in the process of getting a divorce now," Harvey

Harvey Black

mused, " but I want another wife. I'm old fashioned. I have to marry them." He pushed his cap back off the long, red hair that matched the color of his handlebar mustache.

"I'd like to find a 45- to 57-year-old lady in good health who can cook and garden, enjoys traveling, likes adventure and has a pension to match mine." He reeled off the requirements as though he'd listed them before.

I thought of a number of my single friends—some who had never married, others who were widowed or divorced— who met Harvey's qualifications. It didn't take me long to decide that I knew no woman who would want to settle down for a long dark winter of reading, drinking, and watching television in Eagle.

Last year's newspapers and magazines were stacked high inside Harvey's cabin. "Many Alaskans save their reading for the long, dark, cold winter," he explained.

Then he changed the subject to the idea of living elsewhere. "I could sell this cabin for $45,000, but what would I buy with the money? A motor home, perhaps."

Harvey seemed lonely and restless, and he was tired of putting wood on the fire every four or five hours. He was ready to move.

"Not only is firing a stove a lot of work, it's expensive," he said. "Wood can cost up to $90 a cord if we have it hauled in."

Harvey thought his trading business would bring adventure and profit. He had found some of the excitement but not enough profit. Now he was ready to start anew in a warmer climate; only he couldn't seem to figure out how to finance the move.

As we started to leave, he pulled a card out of his pocket. "Let me give you my address so you can let me know if you find this lady I'm looking for," he said.

Still in Eagle

Dave and I both love to read and we think of libraries as primary sources of information. So after talking to Harvey Black, we wandered back to Eagle's log cabin library and social center where we met Carol and Loren Pahlke.

"We chose Eagle because it's the end of the road," Carol said.

"Actually the reasons are much more complex than that," explained her husband, Loren, an anthropologist.

The young couple from Colorado were spending a year in Eagle to study the effect that the closing of the road by snow in the winter has on the 140 or more year-round residents of the community. Although the Pahlkes had been in town less than a week, they had immediately volunteered their services.

"We were given a five minute instruction course," Carol said, "and already we're librarians."

There didn't seem to be enough shelves for all of the books in the library, but Carol said there were even fewer shelves in the cabin they'd rented for the year. She said she'd been struggling to find places to put their books and other belongings they'd brought with them. There was no electricity or plumbing, and they'd been trying to do their laundry in a bucket by hand with a toilet plunger.

The Pahlkes were finding domestic inconveniences a challenge, but as social scientists they were delighted to have a change of pace and were enjoying 4th of July festivities with the town folks. They were actually looking forward to the surprises of the coming winter.

Curious, we called Loren and Carol via Helmers' satellite telephone service one frigid February evening from a hotel room in Anchorage.

"Eagle is nice for a year," Loren said, "but we don't want to stay here. We do, however, want to stay in Alaska so we're looking at the possibility of getting jobs in Anchorage. I miss large libraries and not having easy access to our family and friends in Colorado."

But did they get cabin fever?

"We've been too busy for that," Loren said. "We've done some dog mushing, and we've found the winter rather mild."

Loren did learn something about himself, however. He said he found it difficult to manage his time in Eagle. Because others there weren't on a strict schedule, he had difficulty disciplining himself to get his own work done.

Eagle had been an educational experience for the Pahlkes. Observing how other folks really manage in one of North America's few remaining outposts helped them put into focus their own lifestyle needs and wants. Dave and I envied them their year in Eagle and wondered how we'd manage our time and resources if we chose to spend a year there.

Peace and poultry

"I came looking for gold, but I didn't find it," Dale Reikert told me. "But I found something better—peace and tranquility."

Dale and his wife Gloria were living the simple life in

Eagle, and unlike Loren and Carol Pahlke, we supposed they would probably remain in or near the village.

"We don't need much," Dale explained. "We can live on $1,400 a year up here. We raise chickens and turkeys, plant a garden, can salmon and put potatoes up for the winter."

As we talked, a dozen newly hatched turkeys fluttered and scratched in the back of a child's-size rusty red wagon. "If the turkeys survive, we'll have poultry to eat this winter," Gloria said.

Gloria and Dale moved to Eagle from Saginaw, Michigan after their ambition for material success vanished in flames one terrible night as their "ma and pa" grocery story burned to the ground.

"We used to watch a lot of TV when we had the store," Gloria said. "Now we don't even own a TV. When we went back Outside to visit our children, we got hooked again on the tube. We were glad to get back here and forget television. It took up too much of our time."

I could understand TV taking up too much time.

Dale and Gloria were busying themselves with other projects in Alaska. During the winter they planned to carry salvaged lumber to an isolated place several miles from town where they would build a cabin the following summer. Meanwhile, they were making their home in a ramshackle rented place near the riverfront.

"It's a good house," Dale said optimistically pointing to their windowless plywood and tarpaper shack. "If there was more insulation in the walls, we wouldn't have to burn so much wood; but we keep warm."

"In Alaska no one has to be in a rush to do anything," Gloria added. "People back home are always hurrying to get somewhere."

They'll build their new cabin eventually, but there's no compulsion or pressure to "do it now." Dale and Gloria have few material needs. They left a busy city with TV and lots of automobiles. They've traded a grocery store for a vegetable garden and exchanged customers and neighbors for a few chickens and turkeys. They're making the kind of life that pleases them, and they have each other.

"Gold is where you find it," Dale said. "So are peace and freedom."

Log cabin life

The Reikerts feel they've found the good life. But the good life can be elusive even in the legendary Alaskan bush, as Karen Kallen-Brown discovered.

We spotted Karen and Randy Brown loading a canoe on the banks of the Yukon River which runs along the north side of Eagle. Karen came to Alaska to teach after graduation from an eastern college. She came with great expectations but found herself teaching in a one-room school in an Alaskan bush village—with seven students in grades five to seven.

How exciting to teach in a bush village and to have only seven students, I thought. Karen didn't agree. She explained that five of her pupils needed special education, that it took her all year to get them tested and that she had a hard time surviving, physically, herself.

"It was an ordeal just sorting through my boxes of supplies to find materials for the students to use," she said. "And there was no place to live. I moved my boxes and bed roll eight times that year, finally ended up living in a room in the town jail. There just wasn't adequate housing where I could unpack my belongings and feel either that I wasn't intruding or being intruded upon.

"In addition, cutting wood to keep me warm was taking all of my leisure time," Karen said glancing at Randy who was loading fishing tackle into the canoe. "Finally, I wrote to Randy who was living in a cabin in the woods near the Yukon River. I told him, "You'll have to come and cut wood for me or I can't make it through the winter. I just can't cut wood and teach, too.""

Karen and Randy Brown pack their canoe.

This "far out" teaching job just wasn't the answer for Karen; however, Randy did come and cut wood for her, and she finished the school year and then quit. When we first met them along the Yukon, she and Randy had chosen, for the present, to be among the "river people" who live off the river and the land, fishing for salmon and picking berries. The optimistic young couple were expecting to can ninety jars of salmon to see them through the cold months and they were going to preserve berries in honey.

During the winter, both planned to produce crafts. Randy would make wooden bowls to sell in local stores and Karen would weave rugs and wall hangings for their newly built 20 x 20-foot cabin. When she had completed enough items for their home, she said she might weave to sell.

"I want to create something that's useful—not just decorative," Randy explained when we asked him why he didn't make the kind of wooden ornaments found in the shops that cater to tourists.

Randy said he had been comfortable in his 8 x 8-foot cabin near Eagle, but that Karen had insisted that they needed more room. As a result, they'd built the larger cabin on a secluded bank of the Yukon, a few miles upriver from the town.

"I want to live where I can't see any neighbors," Karen explained.

I could understand that. We had built our house back in the woods out of view from the road. But there are nearly a dozen houses within a mile. We don't see our neighbors often, but we know we can count on them when necessary. And sometimes we have a neighborhood potluck. Live up the river? I don't think I'd like that. I would like to live near water, however.

As we talked, Randy and Karen packed their gear and supplies into a canoe which they planned to float down the river to a better fishing spot. They'd fish for salmon, getting enough for themselves and more to barter with friends for other necessities. It would be a physically rugged summer, but Karen and Randy appeared to be ready. There was no look of hurry or pressure. They were doing something they enjoyed and were self-sufficient and contented. We hoped that, next spring when the ice finally broke up on the river, they'd still be as happy.

When we returned to Eagle five years later, we learned that Jedediah Aspen Kallen-Brown had arrived and was now toddling around the new cabin that Karen and Randy had built within the village of Eagle. Karen had been teaching in Eagle while Randy cared for Jedediah as well as designing and building birch bark canoes and baskets.

Randy's craftsmanship is excellent, so good in fact that one of his canoes had been commissioned by the state museum in Anchorage. He was now building another canoe for the Eagle museum and hoped to obtain contracts to build additional "authentic" replicas.

Karen was enjoying teaching more than before.

"I needed a steady job to repay my college loans and build

this house," she said. But it was obvious that she was enjoying it. She and her students had been exchanging letters with pupils from the Lower 48. Karen explained that the students

Randy and Karen Brown enjoy life with Jedediah.

had learned mapping, writing and graphing in the process. They'd sent Eagle memorabilia, *Alaska* magazines, seashells and rocks to the students with whom they corresponded. In return, they had received T-shirts, postcards and magazines from many states.

During the summers, Karen and Randy continued to fish for salmon. They were now canning it with a pressure cooker. A root cellar beneath a trap door in their living room provides year-round refrigeration. Although they had neither running water nor indoor toilet, the 18 x 18-foot, one-room log cabin appeared very comfortable.

Karen said that the biggest challenge when they lived in the bush year around was winter travel. "It was 56 degrees below zero when we made a trip to town from the bush cabin to replenish supplies," she said. "We didn't dare stop moving. I had to rely on Randy and a commerical hand warmer to keep from freezing. It took us eight days to make the trek from Eagle to our house in the bush."

Karen planned to fly back to the bush cabin at Christmas time. It would cost her $175 to pay the pilot, but it would be necessary because her vacation time from teaching would be limited. Randy would leave several weeks ahead of her taking with him a toboggan and four dogs.

The thought of cold weather treks didn't appeal to me. I certainly hoped that Dave wasn't thinking about doing anything like that. It's one thing to hike the Chilkoot Trail in June, even with snow still in the pass. Quite another to mush a toboggan and dog team through the snow at 56 degrees below zero.

Karen's parents from New Jersey were visiting the young family in their new home. Her mother was worried about medical emergencies.

"There are risks here," Karen admitted. "But Jed was born in Anchorage. We have people here in Eagle with emergency medical training. We have radios and we practice preventive medicine."

Besides the necessary services that most of us take for granted, I thought I would miss the theatre, art galleries and concerts.

"Sure I miss ballet," Karen said as though reading my thoughts. "We can't always get into Anchorage when the symphony or ballet is there."

It took time for Karen and Randy to get settled into a routine that pleased them, but they appeared happy. Their charming log cabin was to be envied by many romantic adventurers, including Dave and me, who have dreamed of living on the edge of the frontier.

Living along the river

"There are few hours in life more agreeable than the hour dedicated to the ceremony known as afternoon tea," wrote American novelist and essayist Henry James.

This statement took on new meaning for us as Dave and I spent a pleasant afternoon drinking tea with Terry and Mary Anne McMullin in their mobile home while they told us their life story.

Terry was principal of the school in the Indian village just outside of Eagle. Linda, at the Eagle's Nest, had suggested we look up Terry and Mary Anne. We later learned that the McMullins' daughter worked part-time as a waitress at the restaurant.

At the McMullins' we sat at the tiny table in one of the two house trailers in which the couple and their children lived while they completed a cabin nearby that would be their new home. Stacks of lumber and bales of insulation surrounded the trailers. "The new cabin will be finished before winter," Terry said. "Here there's a time and a season for everything. I keep starting projects before I complete the ones I'm working on, but we have to fish while the salmon are running. We'll get back to working on the cabin when the salmon runs are over."

The McMullins' children attend the Indian village school where their father is principal. "But the village is dying," Terry said. "The young people go Outside as soon as they can. Some survive there; others return and take up the bottle."

It was hard for us to imagine growing up in a community with no traffic lights, expressways or shopping malls. After a lifetime of subsistance hunting and fishing, it could be a shock to suddenly find oneself dependent upon a supermarket. How would it feel to be confronted for the first time with 4,000 food items from which to choose? How could a person find a job or purchase an automobile if he'd never even driven one? Or learn to use public transportation in a strange land?

To suddenly find themselves thrust into a metropolis was more of a cultural shock than some of the youths from the frontier could face.

It's difficult for most of us to imagine that other people haven't had the same experiences we've had. Somehow we expect that everyone we meet can empathize with us about our situations. No wonder there's a lack of communication between peoples of the world.

Yet, on the other hand, sometimes I think it's amazing how many of the same experiences and feelings are shared by many of us. A desire to do something different, and to try something that everyone else isn't doing may not be universal, but it's perhaps more common than many of us might think.

Terry and Mary Anne were two such people. Terry had taught school in Eagle in the 1960's before the couple left to live on the river with their four children. In this way, their lives resembled Karen and Randy Brown's.

"The river was a great place to raise our kids," Mary Anne said, "because we were constantly together. We got to know one another better. We taught the kids at home by correspondence. They worked three hours a day on their lessons."

"Only three hours a day?" I questioned.

"Three hours doesn't sound like much," Terry added, "but when you don't take time out for physical education, lunch and recesses, that's quite a bit of study time."

"The kids were never bored in the bush," added Mary Anne. "They had plenty to do—just helping us keep food on the table and getting firewood for the stove. They read a lot and they were always exploring. We often had to go and look for them when it got dark. They also helped us take care of the sled dogs."

"We used the dogs on our trap lines," Terry explained. "We still keep about 20 dogs—for fun and sport now, but on the river they were a necessity."

As Dave and I left the McMullins' trailer, we noticed the

dogs tied up along the edge of the woods.

"They won't bother you if you're not afraid of them," Mary Anne assured us. We decided, however, we'd not like to encounter the dogs without their owners near by.

Terry and Mary Anne found a peace on the river that doesn't exist in more populated areas; but after awhile they felt it was time to return to society. So they went back to Eagle and Terry began teaching again.

"Teachers' pay is good in Alaska, but the turnover is constant," Terry told us.

"Why the big turnover?" I asked.

"Problems are magnified in a small community," he said. "We live so close together here. There's nowhere to go to escape other people—even for a weekend. Flying out is very expensive. So we stay and sometimes that's stifling."

Isolation, we were learning, is relative.

When we returned to Eagle five years later, we noticed many changes. A nice restaurant on the river front was owned and operated by the McMullins' daughter and her husband. They featured an extensive oriental menu and had hired a young Chinese couple as cook and waitress for the summer. The Oriental woman said, "My husband and I plan to open a restaurant of our own in New York City, Seattle or San Francisco; meanwhile, we are enjoying our time here."

The McMullins' daughter and husband were also building a motel behind the restaurant which would serve tourists, and they operated a small grocery next door to the restaurant.

Salmon steaks

The McMullins live in Eagle year round. Others, like Jessie and Kathryn Knight from Kansas City, Missouri, are summer residents.

"I've been busy today," Jessie said, as he sliced a full cross section from an enormous silver salmon and handed it to me. I thanked him and held the huge fish while he carved off

Jesse Knight slices salmon steaks.

another thick steak.

It was now after 9 a. m. and the townsfolk were just beginning to stir.

"Yes, I've already been fishing this morning," Jessie explained. "Sometimes I put my net into the river two or three times a day."

Jessie's wife Kathryn was busy building up steam in the pressure cooker and would soon be canning some of the salmon. Outside, Jessie was sharing much of his morning's catch with neighbors and visitors.

The couple lived upstairs in a quaint, old river front building which Jessie was attempting to restore. Formerly a store and warehouse, the structure held an excitement for Jessie and he was fascinated with the prospect of renovating it—especially since it stood next door to the historical museum.

"I enjoy working on this old store," he said. "It's going to cost a lot to fix it up though. Because it's a historic structure, I could get help from the government; but I'd have to give up my rights to the building, so I'm doing it myself."

Independence was obviously important to Jessie, and the restoration work, we decided, was therapy for him. But, meanwhile, every day there were fish in the Yukon River that had to be caught.

We put Jessie's salmon steaks into our cooler and that evening pan fried them over our Coleman stove and declared them the tenderest, most moist and most flavorful fish we had ever eaten.

During dinner, we thought about Jessie and his renovation project. He was in no hurry to complete the work on the building. Whether he finished it that year or the next wouldn't really matter. What mattered was that Jessie and Kathryn liked what they were doing. They were contented with their life.

Being able to appreciate the process rather than to look only toward the end result is important. Some of us take longer than others to learn this lesson. If we look ahead only to the destination of a trip, the journey can become drudgery and the destination often disappointing.

I was beginning to learn on this trip the importance of savoring each moment. Dave and I were traveling with no time schedule in mind. There was no reason to hurry and leave a place that we were enjoying.

People like the Browns, McMullins and Knights have found peace in the wilderness. But what really draws people to the tiny village of Eagle? When we met Sharon and Steve Hamilton in the library, I asked them this question.

"People come to Eagle because it's the end of the road," Sharon offered, repeating a reason we'd heard before.

"Some people want to live here, but they find they can't," Steve added. "Men love it here, but it's tough on women. Most men trap and mine and fish. The women are often left home cutting wood and stoking the fire."

Steve traps for furs, does general repair work and painting in the neighborhood, cultivates gardens in the summer and serves occasionally as a missionary preacher.

"When I have to be gone from home for any length of time, I make sure Sharon has enough fuel, water and electricity," Steve said. "This shows her that I care. Sure, I could make more money if I'd go to work on the North Slope in the oil fields—or in the gold mine, but I think our family relationship is more important than money. I believe if a fellow spends his time away from home, he makes relationships where he is—and the marriage suffers."

Again in 1986 I met Steve and Sharon in the library. This time they wanted to borrow the Polaroid camera which the library usually has available for loan. Alas, the camera was away for repairs. So I volunteered to take the photo which Sharon and Steve wanted. Someone was collecting photos of many churches in Alaska and had asked for a snapshot of the

Missionary work, home and family are important to Sharon and Steve Hamilton.

church in Eagle. I walked over to the church where a Bible School was in process, posed Sharon and Steve in front of the building and snapped their photo.

Meanwhile I learned that while I was back in Michigan, Steve had done construction work in Palmer for two years. The couple rented a house there and the kids went to a larger school in Palmer. Now the family is back in Eagle, trapping and hunting, and Steve serves as part-time volunteer minister.

"No, we don't have a lot of income," Steve said. "But we don't need a lot. We own our home here and we don't have many expenses."

Recipe for comfortable living

The Helmers at the general store in Eagle told us about Diana and Jack Green. "Since you're a writer, you'll want to meet Diana," Sue Helmer said. "Diana's a writer too."

We followed Sue's directions and found a large, new, very modern cabin in the woods. It was dinner time so I suggested we'd go for a walk and return later, but the Greens insisted that we come in and have dessert with them. Diana had prepared a delightful apple and lemon custard, and I came away with the recipe for the dessert and a respect for her reputation as a gourmet cook.

"We decided we preferred to be on the periphery of society looking in," explained Jack, who had been a microwave engineer in Colorado before coming to Alaska.

"Yes, we want to choose the parts of society in which we participate," added Diana whose black hair was pulled back smartly. She would have looked sharp anywhere. Here, she looked comfortable in designer blue jeans and classic shirt, but I surmised she would be equally at home in Manhattan wearing a tweed suit and silk blouse.

Although Diana and Jack were enjoying the isolation of Eagle, they usually spent several of the winter months in Hawaii. "We work six months and play six months," was the way Jack put it.

The Greens' newly-built log home in Eagle is secluded, like Eagle itself, at the end of its own narrow dirt road back into the spruce forest about a mile from the town. The home is no wilderness cabin by bush standards, but quite modern, with most of the conveniences. The Greens heat their home with wood, their plumbing is indoors and their diesel-powered generator keeps them independent from Helmer's Electric Company.

Diana, a freelance writer who earned a doctorate in classical languages from the University of Colorado, grew up in upstate New York as Jack had. "I just wanted to be well-educated," she explained when asked what particular plans she had for her classical language training.

Since the couple moved to Alaska in 1975, Diana has self-published two cookbooks emphasizing recipes with natural foods. She has also been a correspondent for an Anchorage newspaper and she published a newsletter entitled *The Organic Gourmet*. These activities provided her with ways to promote her cookbooks as well as an outlet for her creativity. When we talked to her, she was writing a gourmet foods column for *The Anchorage Times* and working on a third cookbook.

Her specialities included sauteed tofu with seasoned bread crumbs, apple baked beets, ginger glazed carrots and pumpkin dinner rolls.

"I've learned to cook without sugar, refined flour or hydrogenated fats," she explained.

In her popular breakfast cookbook entitled *Sunrise*, she tells readers how to make granola thirteen ways, how to prepare more than 50 kinds of pancakes including crepes, blintzes and flapjacks and how to bake 30 kinds of muffins, bread and rolls.

"I became interested in natural foods as a matter of necessity when I knew we were coming to Alaska," Diana said. "I imagined us totally independent out in the bush."

As it turned out, most basic supplies were available from local stores, but food preservation skills have been very useful. The day before we visited with them, Diana had cleaned a number of geese for their freezer. Preserving food seemed a compulsion for the Greens.

In Eagle, the couple was secluded, yet not really isolated—except as they chose to be. Jack managed a gold mine from May until September although he had had a number of jobs since coming to Alaska, including hauling gravel and operating a construction company. Diana taught school for several years.

"We lived in a tent the first summer we were here while we

built a one-room cabin," Diana recalled.

"Alaska is a wide open country where a man can be free," said Jack, "—free from government regulations."

The population density in Alaska is less than one person per ten square miles, yet many present residents aren't inviting any more settlers. Although there are wide open spaces, people such as Jack and Diana discourage newcomers.

"We really can't handle any more people right here," Diana said. "There's not enough fuel, timber or game; nor are there enough trapping, fishing and mining spaces."

"The gold mining territory is all legally staked out," Jack added. "The best hunting, fishing and trapping areas have been claimed. Everybody knows where the others work, and they don't interfere."

Jack and Diana were living out their frontier dream, but they feared their own freedom and independence might be threatened if too many others decided that this is the place to be free and independent.

New interests beckoned the Greens, however; and when we returned to Eagle five years later, we learned they had moved to Oregon. Diana, we were told, was taking post graduate courses and wanted to get back into teaching and research, and Jack had purchased a computer and was interested in programming for industry.

John Borg, postmaster at Eagle, said, "I believe they needed new challenges that Eagle wouldn't provide."

The postmaster

"You must be the couple from Kalamazoo," said John Borg when we entered the post office. It seemed that the news had traveled quickly over the community grapevine.

John Borg came North while he was in the U. S. military service. He remained in Alaska and was a mail carrier in Anchorage from 1961 to 1968. Then he came to Eagle where he operated a roadhouse for five years until becoming postmaster in 1973.

His wife Betty, who grew up in Alaska, volunteers in the small public library, sells vitamins and plays a guitar. While we were in town she was busy preparing for a white elephant sale for the 4th of July festival.

John Borg

John is chairman of the board at church. He spoke freely from his window at the post office and seemed to like talking with visitors. Betty was a little more hesitant and didn't wish to be quoted. She and some residents of Eagle felt they had been "burned" by earlier writers and so were reluctant to pour out their life stories. I could understand how they felt. Although only a minority of reporters emphasize the sensational, a person who has been misquoted previously could certainly be expected to be cautious about what they say.

Gold is where you find it

"If you want to live in Alaska, bring a cook--one who is a good companion," Tim Ingraham advised us.

Dave and I met Tim in the Eagle's Nest restaurant on our second morning in Eagle. He was wearing a cowboy hat and boots, and if we hadn't known better, we'd have thought we were in Colorado or Montana.

The 36-year old gold miner was working that summer with a crew of three other men. For Tim, the appeal of Alaska was that he could be on his own as much as he wished. "Many folks think they can live off the land, but they can't," he said. "They don't realize what they're getting into by going to live and work in the bush. The isolation can be unbearable.

"But if you insist on coming, plan for the worst. And remember that 'to get hurt or get sick out in the bush is to die.' That's what the Indians say."

It was obvious that Tim didn't expect to get sick or injured. It was also obvious that he delighted in playing the macho sourdough role for us cheechakos.

Since work in the gold mines is seasonal, Tim planned on making gold jewelry the following winter. "At least I'm going to give it a try," he said. "No, I've never made jewelry before, but I'll learn the skills. If others can do it, so can I."

It's this willingness to adapt and to try something new that is typical of the people we found as we traveled around the state of Alaska.

"It's not what you know, but it's who you know here that's important," Tim said. He was working for wages, but he also had permission from his employers to work the claim on his own time and keep what he found.

The gold rush stampeders of 1898 toted their nuggets in cloth sacks. Modern miners often carry their prized samples in tiny plastic pill vials with child-proof caps.

Dave and I had tried our hands at panning for gold on Bonanza Creek near Dawson City, Yukon. We told Tim we had some bright flecks of something we had carefully sifted from the source of the big gold strikes which had occurred more than 80 years earlier. I spread out the contents of our plastic film can on the table and asked him what gold really looks like.

"Like this," Tim said, pulling his pill vial from a breast pocket. Pushing aside his coffee mug, he spread out about half an ounce of small nuggets and flakes on a paper napkin.

"All that glitters isn't gold," he said. He explained about mica and pyrites and showed us how a gentle breath would blow away most of our "find," leaving a small particle of gold he had placed amidst our "flakes of nothing."

I remembered interviewing rockhounds in Michigan and hearing about "fool's gold." My friends used to invite me to join their rockhound club. Geology has always fascinated me, but I hadn't thought I had time for that hobby. I began to think I should have made time.

"Now, you have some *real* gold," Tim said, dumping the napkinful of particles into the plastic film can in which we had collected our gold.

Tim told us he had lived in Wrangell, in the Southeast panhandle, before drifting northward to Eagle. When he wanted work, he headed off among the tailings of former claims along the creeks and turbid tributaries of the Yukon. Although he may not spend the rest of his life mining gold, Tim will probably be happy doing whatever work he chooses. His positive attitude was appealing. Here was someone cheerfully adapting to the climate, to the seasons and to the work available.

As I listened to Tim, I thought about the urgency of finding a job for myself if we moved North. I wondered if I could be as adaptable. I decided I might have to accept less than I wanted—and to be prepared for the worse, yet not dwell on it. What I was learning from the people we'd talked to was to savor the moment, enjoy the scenery. I made up my mind that I'd wait and deal with underemployment—or a fall over the cliff if and when it happened—but not before. I decided that maybe it was worth coming all of these miles just to be able to begin to adopt this pragmatic philosophy of life.

Shopkeepers

We left The Eagle's Nest and went back toward Helmers'

general store. Across the street was a new business operated by two women, Pat and Lou.

We ambled into the little store where Lou sold groceries from spartanly stocked shelves in one part of the building and Pat created caribou rings and other novelties for their craft shop next door.

The short summer is tourist time when local artisans hope to sell the products of their dark winter days. Makeshift display cases were filled with beadwork necklaces, wood carvings and a variety of other items in the shop Pat and Lou named "The River's Edge."

The two women, both divorced, lived with their children in an apartment upstairs. Both former wives of career Army men, Pat and Lou were friends when their ex-husbands were stationed together in Missouri. They came to Eagle to visit, fell in love with the town, moved here and opened a store. Now, a block from the rushing Yukon, these two enterprising women had risked their savings in exchange for a chance to find peace and pleasure in a land they love.

"It's the quality of life we've found here that's important," Pat said, putting down her chain saw. She had just finished cutting fifteen cords of wood for their winter heating supply. "The people are friendly here. They all pitch in and help one another. Folks here helped us put insulation in our house and store."

In addition to their shop, Pat and Lou had acquired the contract to make the regular mail run from the airport to the post office. Dave and I happened to be in the post office when the two women had arrived the day before with their van full of mail. Nearly everyone in the village turned out to meet them, and they all waited patiently while the mail was sorted and put into the boxes by Postmaster Borg.

Pat told us she planned to apply for substitute teaching to supplement their joint incomes. "I'm impressed with the school system here," she said. "The teachers really care about their students. They go with them on nature hikes, play volleyball with them and take them on stargazing excursions.

"The ratio of pupils to teachers is eight to one," she said. "This not only makes it easier for teachers to offer individual attention but also enables them to get to know each student personally.

"Few winter activities compete with school for the children's time, but when there's a social activity, everyone takes part," Pat added. She described a recent party up the river where the whole town took food and musical instruments and, as Pat put it, "had a ball."

"People need one another here in Eagle," she said. "Individuals who probably would never get acquainted in another time and place become friends here and help one another."

We knew what Pat meant, for in less than forty-eight hours it seemed that we had met half the town. Somehow we felt we belonged in Eagle—that we could return and they'd be glad to see us—like old friends.

But there was much more ground we wanted to cover. So after spending some time at Eagle's annual community Fourth of July parade and carnival, for which some of the Indian children dressed up like—well, yes, Indians—we headed south toward the Alaska Highway junction near Tok. As we left Eagle, I calculated the distance to Tok. It would be 172 miles. Doing some more figuring, I decided we were about 106 miles from a spot on the map marked Chicken.

Fourth of July in Eagle is a community affair.

Tok

At a bookshop in Dawson City, Yukon, the proprietor had sold us a copy of *Tisha,* the story of the experiences of a young teacher in the Alaskan bush back in the 1920s

"*Tisha* means *teacher,*" explained the bookseller as she slipped the paperback into a paper bag. "You know, Ann Purdy, the heroine of this book, still lives over in Chicken, and they say she likes to have visitors."

We found out that Mrs. Purdy lived in a yellow house at the end of the narrow dirt road by the post office. The town of Chicken appeared to consist of a grocery, a tavern, an airport and a gas station. According to *The Milepost,* the gas station owner will open up at night for emergencies. I hoped we didn't have any emergencies—least of all at night.

The town had been named Chicken, so the story goes, because the area contained many wild ptarmigan; settlers wanted to name the area for the bird, but were unable to spell *ptarmigan* so they settled for *Chicken,* the common name for ptarmigan.

After locating the tiny post office, we followed the route as we had been instructed and also spotted a hand lettered sign stating that Ann Purdy would enjoy company. We followed the arrows to her modest cabin at the end of the road.

The door stood open and sounds of laughter and conversation filled the warm July evening. A dozen of Ann's foster children had come home for the holiday. (Ann had made a home for many children throughout the years.) She invited us inside like a member of her family. When we asked her to autograph our paperback copy of *Tisha,* she smiled and asked, "Would you like to see the hard cover edition?"

What could we say?

She reached into a convenient carton and proudly handed us a mint copy complete with dust jacket. We bought it, of course, and asked her to autograph and inscribe it as a gift for my daughter, Marcia.

We didn't stay long because Ann was enjoying a rare visit with her family, but we did remain long enough to learn that she had been having difficulty with her co-author and publisher. It seems that *Tisha* was to have been an "as told to" autobiography, but Ann said that the book turned out like a romance novel and that it was published without her name as author.

"I'm writing another book about my life," she said. "This time it will have *my* name on it."

Tok Junction

As we left Chicken, we realized it would soon be time to eat again, and although we sometimes bought food and picnicked, we found that some of our best opportunities to gather information were at eating establishments.

Joyce was waiting tables and her husband was head cook at the restaurant in Tok where we stopped to have dinner. The newlywed couple had come to Anchorage from Kalispell, Montana for what they referred to as a five-year "working vacation." During that time Joyce completed a degree in social work.

I remembered the summers I'd spent waiting tables back in St. Johns, Michigan while working on a teaching degree during the school year. I could do it again, I thought— if we were to move to Alaska.

"Anchorage will be a compromise for us," Joyce said. "Eventually we'll move back to the city and take jobs in the fields for which we trained, but we needed to get away from our families for awhile. So did my sister. She and her family followed us to Alaska, but they've already gone back Outside.

"Some folks get disillusioned about Alaska," Joyce explained. "They want to build a log cabin and live in the forest. But soon they miss the conveniences and learn that what they really want to do is just look at log cabins but live in the city."

Although I have lived in a rural area most of my life, I wondered whether I was really a country person—or a city person. Primitive living just might not be what I was looking for.

Next to the restaurant stood the Burnt Paw gift shop. The showcase was filled with Indian and Eskimo jewelry and souvenir carvings from soapstone, jade and wood. On the wall hung an Iditarod dog sled race poster. The nearby postcard rack was filled with photographs of dog teams in action, fireweed in blossom, snow capped mountains and the popular outdoorsman's joke, a fur bearing fish.

Margie was standing behind the glass counter. "My husband had a dream to go to Alaska, so when he got a job, we came," Margie explained. "He and his son do construction work. His son continues indoor building while my husband and I spend the winter in Chicken."

"In Chicken?" I gasped. "Whatever do you do there all winter?"

"My husband traps; I read a lot and I've learned to crochet," Margie answered. "I drink coffee with friends and plan dinner parties. We have 200 pounds of halibut to use up this year. We buy our supplies for the winter in Anchorage when they have a 'stock up' sale."

Apparently Alaska hadn't been part of Margie's dreams, but she's here because her husband is, and she has adapted. She has found things to do and she'll probably stay in Alaska as long as her husband wants to, but she won't be particularly upset if they ever decide to go back Outside.

I was reminded of how the destiny of so many women is shaped by the plans of the men they marry. Had I married a man whose goals I share? I hoped so. I'd needed to prove that I could make it on my own after my divorce so that I would feel good about myself, but I thought about how many women I know who have no identity of their own.

When I was growing up, many young women's chief goal was to find a husband. They chose their colleges and the cities where they took jobs according to the likelihood of meeting and marrying a desirable male.

In the 1980s, most of us have decided that each woman must be prepared to make her own way. Maybe she won't have to support herself, but it certainly will improve her self-image if she has proven to herself that she can. And perhaps she won't have to remain trapped in an unhappy or undesirable marriage just because she feels that she wouldn't be able to manage on her own.

Of course, there are trade-offs. Even today most married women defer to their husbands' careers. I'm not so sure that the next generation will do that. I see more young couples sharing home and child rearing responsibilities than ever before.

Dave usually does the dishes after I've cooked a meal. I do the laundry and he takes care of automobile things like rotating tires and changing the oil. If the decision arises—to go or not to go to live in Alaska— I'm confident that we'll make the decision together.

The Right Stuff

Since we were near Tok, I decided it was time to try to contact David and Kathy Cramer.

"When you get to Alaska, look up David Cramer," urged my friend Nancy Stryker. "We grew up together and David needed more space around him than the rest of us did."

I found a phone booth at a tourist information center and called Kathy. She invited us to their home for dinner that evening. I was glad we had taken Nancy's suggestion, for the Cramers welcomed us and reinforced our instant good feelings about Alaska.

A holstered handgun was slung on a wooden peg beside the back door. Four rifles were racked on the wall ready for use. A ram's head, a fox pelt and a bearskin rug helped complete the decor of David and Kathy Cramer's neatly kept cabin deep in the spruce forest 40 miles south of the Alaska Highway junction at Tok.

Their home is comfortable by any standard, yet not filled with some of the conveniences taken for granted in the Lower 48. Book shelves lined one wall of the cabin and wooden fuel oil crates served as file cabinets for the office of Summit Construction Company, the Cramers' thriving business.

The lights in their home were fueled by propane gas and so was their food freezer. Drinking water was pumped through a hose from a nearby creek, using electricity from their own gasoline powered generator which runs only an hour or two each day. Fortunately, the stream continues to flow beneath a thick layer of ice even during the coldest weather.

Mail is delivered twice a week to their box in town, but there's no school nearby so Kathy taught their six-year-old son Eric by correspondence. Boxes of books arrived each month from the Fairbanks Public Library for Eric and two-year-old Mara.

"We tell the librarians the categories we're interested in and they send us a dozen books a month," Kathy explained.

Kathy Cramer orders library books by mail for Eric and Mara.

"All we have to do is pay the return postage."

One of the books on the shelf was Tom Wolfe's *The Right Stuff.* Although the book is about Navy fliers and astronauts, it didn't take long to realize that the Cramers, too, are pioneers who possess some of the *right stuff.*

"There are people who talk about doing something," David said, "and there are others who just go and do it. If you can leave the known and come to the unknown, you can learn most anything—how to run a fishing boat, drive a tractor, build a cabin—whatever skills you need."

I wondered whether my Dave and I would fall into the category of talkers—or if we'd be considered doers. This trip had required considerable planning and commitment; and we thought we were seriously considering starting a new life together here on the frontier. Or were we just talking about it?

Here we were listening to Alaskans talking about living in Alaska. Would we be willing to burn our bridges behind us? Would we have to make such a major move to "make it" in the eyes of people like David Cramer? Or would it be necessary for us to come as far as Alaska to prove something about ourselves? I left that question unanswered and directed my attention to our host.

David Cramer's interest in the out-of-doors led him to a college degree in biology and a job, for a short time, as a wildlife management officer. His preoccupation with outdoor life had begun when he was a kid in Kalamazoo. "My parents gave us a few rules when we were kids," he said. "They told us to watch out for snakes. So we did, and we brought them home whenever we found them."

Reportedly, there are no snakes in Alaska, but there are plenty of challenges and adventures, and David and Kathy Cramer have faced their share. After eight years, the Cramers said they wouldn't want to live anywhere else.

David Cramer was graduated from the University of Colorado in 1970 and headed north with his friend, Stan Koster, two pack horses and a pickup truck. They intended to homestead in Canada, but regulations covering foreign nationals in British Columbia convinced the two young men they should move on to Alaska.

Stan was later drafted into the army, but David stayed on and worked in Alaska, fishing for salmon and crab and later operating heavy equipment for a gold mine.

David and Kathy met while he was home on a visit to Michigan. She followed him back to Alaska and took a job in a cannery.

Feeling the need for marketable skills, David looked for a vocation that would leave him independent and free from desk work. He had no experience with carpentry, but he chose it anyway. He learned the building trades by "just figuring it out," he said, and used his college trigonometry to calculate roof rafter angles.

David has also become versed in plumbing and electrical wiring, and his Summit Construction company became a successful business. He erected several log homes for people in Alaska and completed other projects ranging from installing bulk fuel storage tanks to building an addition to the public school in Eagle.

"We work from seven a. m. until eleven p. m. during the short arctic summer when it never really gets dark," David said. "At best, the outdoor working season is five months long."

Much of their winter travel in the bush is done by snowmobiles, referred to throughout the North as snow machines; and although the weather is usually numbing and often hostile, it's the winter season they enjoy most because winters are family times.

David Cramer

David Cramer gets excited when he talks about the vacation cabin he built. "It's on a secluded lake back in the hills where the four of us can go in and ice fish. In February and March the sun puts out enough heat that we can spend a few hours fishing." Otherwise the cold, dark days are unappealing.

"I don't like wearing a hat, but I have to because of the cold," David said. "At subzero temperatures facial hair freezes to you; your eyelashes stick together and your vision goes.

"And when the temperature drops to 50 below—sometimes as early as Halloween—we have to add wood to the fire every half hour. At night, we fill the stove plumb up; yet it often takes an hour or two in the morning to get the house back up from 45 to 70 degrees." I shivered just thinking of this.

Consequently, the Cramers, like many other Alaskans, burn some fuel oil despite the high cost. And sometimes, when the mercury really bottoms out, no one goes anywhere—except on skis or snowshoes.

"Vehicles are impossible to operate under 50 below," David said. "Sometimes it might be 60 below in the village of Tok for several days—maybe as many as fourteen days. But it usually doesn't get that cold out here at our place."

Adjustment to Alaska has been more difficult for Kathy. Yet she recently turned down her husband's offer to build them a new home in town within easy traveling distance of friends and shopping. They're proud of their well-kept, rustic bush country home and pleased with themselves for improving on the primitive conditions of 1973. "We've a sense of accomplishment that we've managed to stick it out here for eight years," she explained.

But there are trade-offs. "I like to be alone," Kathy said, "but I miss having community things to do. I'd like to take classes in town, but I don't like to think of driving the 80 mile round trip to Tok on winter nights. The terror wins out. I don't take the classes."

But when it comes to the children, Kathy reaches out. "When I go Outside, I take the kids to places like the Kellogg cereal plant in Battle Creek. Eric took swimming lessons at the YWCA while we were in Kalamazoo last summer, and I make sure the kids get to ride on the train and bus as well as having plane rides to and from Kalamazoo. We can fly from Anchorage to Chicago in half a day. We get Outside about every two years, but it's getting more and more expensive."

David Cramer's business takes him to Anchorage, nearly 300 miles away, half a dozen times a year, and sometimes Kathy goes with him to catch up on shopping.

"We buy our groceries in bulk in Anchorage—perhaps five or six hundred dollars at a crack," Kathy related. Her grocery list looks something like this: a case of canned corn, a case of green beans, 100 pounds of white sugar, 25 pounds of brown sugar, one case of powdered milk and twelve boxes of cereal. And I thought I have huge grocery bills. This was something else!

"We buy cheese, eggs and produce in Tok," Kathy added. "I preserve salmon in tins, and David brings home fresh game meat such as moose and big horn sheep." She explained that Alaskan laws permit subsistence hunting by residents and natives and that fish and game officers usually approve of shooting animals in self defense.

David and Kathy Cramer and family enjoy life in the bush.

However, getting the game isn't always the sportsman's paradise that one might think. It, too, requires the *right stuff*. For example, there was the moose in the driveway.

"On my way out with the snow machine one morning, I came face to face with an enormous bull moose," David said. "I barely had time to draw my handgun before the animal attacked the snow machine.

"I expected him to kick with his hind feet like a horse. Instead, he stood up and struck at me with his front hooves. He caught my arm. My gun went into the snow. I was sprawled out on my back trying to protect myself and feel for the gun at the same time. The moose walked all over me, but luckily I was able to pick up the gun and squeeze off the shot that felled him."

A call to the Fish and Game office brought permission to finish off the wounded animal, which David did—only to be confronted by six-year-old Eric who chided him—"But Daddy, it's not moose season!"

Five years later we visited the Cramers again. Since we were last there, David had built a lower level under the main floor of their log home. They've installed a bathroom and hot running water.

Kathy now had a job as a part time computer aide at the nearby elementary school. She had just returned from a three-week writing seminar in Fairbanks and had plans to complete two years of schooling which would result in her obtaining a teaching certificate and a master's degree.

"David and I are a pair," Kathy said. "It's hard to speak as an individual here, but getting a job has helped me to cope. It's important now for me to have something to do out of the house. We don't have the support system of our families here."

"I'm mentally stronger for having been here these years," her husband added. "We advise people to forget about coming to Alaska if they just want high wages. And you can't live off the land here. There's too much competition for trap lines."

There's a definite time to hunt and fish, and it isn't all of the time.

David Cramer is still happy to live and work in Alaska. "If I were in the Lower 48, I wouldn't have time to climb a mountain, walk in to fish or to run trap lines. Part of the attraction here is the well-being I derive from being in a place where I have options.

"In summer we work 15 hours a day. I'm willing to do this working for myself. In winter, it's different. Eric and I can go 80 miles on a snow machine. It's nice and it feels good.

"There was a time when we supported ourselves by trapping," David said. "Now trapping provides us pleasure. But I'm the same person I'd be if I lived in Kalamazoo. I know where I do the best work and sitting in an office isn't it.

"Why am I here?" He repeated my question.

"Economically, I can work half the year. Construction provides an outlet for me as well as an income. There are enough facets to the commercial construction business to be a challenge. Every job is different and interesting enough to justify doing it.

"Going into town is mentally the same thing as going back Outside. There are traffic signals. Yes, I enjoy visiting the folks at home in Michigan, but I don't want to live there. Within a week I'm caught up on what everyone is doing.

"I think it sometimes takes a semi-catastrophic event to help people determine what's not worth the hassle, what's important. When you're alone in isolation, you become introspective. Being alone gives you a chance to think and to understand what you are and what you should be doing. Cities don't provide that environment.

"Isolation gives me a clear understanding of what I should do for the well-being of my own self," David said. "It gives me the courage to accept a challenge and not to worry about the consequences."

Although David seemed to prefer isolation, Kathy sought out friends among her neighbors.

Where cultures meet

One of Kathy's closest friends and—at ten miles away—one of her nearest neighbors is Yvonne Scott. Kathy introduced us when Yvonne dropped off her two-year-old daughter Shelly to stay with Kathy and the children for the day.

Yvonne, a health aide on the Mentasta Indian Reservation about 50 miles southwest of Tok, is in Alaska because that's where her husband Jeff's job is. They moved up from Florida.

"Jeff is a dreamer," Yvonne said. "He came up here to work and he liked it. He's operating heavy equipment for a gold mine about 50 miles into the interior. Since there's no other way to get home except by plane, I see him only about every five weeks. Except for those occasional breaks, he works 12 to 14 hours a day from April until October. But the nice thing is that he's home all winter.

"Jeff runs a trapline, cuts wood and stays home with Shelly," Yvonne said and then added, "I'm independent all summer. Then in the winter I have to become a wife again because Jeff needs to be needed. I like it when he's home, but I make a list of what I'm going to do next summer when he's away at the mine."

I had read that some of the oil drillers and pipeline workers divided their lives between isolated work and distant home and family. It would be like being married to a sailor, I thought. What if Dave—or I—took a job with one of the oil companies at Prudhoe Bay?

Kathy Cramer gave us directions so we could visit Yvonne at the medical clinic on the reservation where she worked.

During the summer, Yvonne's daughter Shelly goes with her mother to the Indian village except for the days when Yvonne has a lot of paperwork to do. Then Shelly stays with a friend.

"Yes, even with Jeff at home, it gets lonely in the winter," sighed Yvonne. "We get cabin fever."

Cabin fever can strike anyone isolated by a severe arctic

winter; the antidote is contact with other people. Dining, dancing, playing cards and other games, putting on a show (or watching one) are some of the ways people keep in touch with the rest of the human race.

One of the centers of action along the Richardson Highway in eastern Alaska is Duffy's Roadhouse at Mile 63. "They show movies at Duffy's every other Friday," Yvonne explained, "and there's always some kind of group meeting there—like Weight Watchers."

Yvonne didn't appear to need Weight Watchers, but I suppose that when there isn't much social activity, one seizes any opportunity for socialization.

"At Duffy's in the evening there are always dogs and children running around, and here are all of these people paying $3 to sit on a hard bench and watch old movies that I've already seen on television in Florida," Yvonne said. "But after a while Duffy's begins to look pretty good, and we look forward to going there just to get out of the house."

The young woman left nursing school in Florida before graduation and came to Alaska to get married. She and Jeff had their wedding reception at Duffy's so the place has an extra special meaning for them.

Yvonne had been working as a health aide at the Indian village. She explained that this job was one usually offered to natives but that none had been willing to train for the position so it was open for her. She had developed a good relationship with her patients. "I try not to make judgments about them and I participate in their activities when they ask me," she explained.

"I was invited to have moose soup at one of the native gatherings," Yvonne recalled. "That was progress, but when I was asked to join the women who were sharing a sauna, I knew I'd 'made it' with them. The women put hot rocks on the floor under a big table, spread blankets over the table and sit naked underneath it and throw water over the hot rocks until steam emerges. It feels good. Some of the women come out occasionally and wash in the cool water with a cloth and then go back in for more steam. Some use soap. Others don't.

"Shelly visits native homes and crawls around wherever the Indian children go. They've even given Shelly an Indian name. When she reaches school age, we may think about moving somewhere else, but I wouldn't hesitate to have her go to school here with the natives."

Yvonne told us about Indian potlatches. "A potlatch is a huge celebration given for funerals and sometimes to express gratitude for something—like for someone whose life was spared. There's much food, lots of dancing and many songs and speeches. Near the end of the event, guns and blankets are passed out to special guests. The chief always seems to receive many guns and blankets.

"The natives here at Mentasta are very clannish," she went on. "They're all related to one another and their values seem very different from ours. They spend what money they have on food, clothing and gas for their cars. They may buy several used autos in one year and discard them when they quit working.

"They don't seem to see the need for saving money and spending it on what we'd consider 'good housing.' Most also prefer to spend money on oil for heating rather than to cut wood."

Free spending isn't unique to native Americans, I thought. I know lots of people who'd rather buy oil than cut wood. Me, for example. Dave, however, enjoys cutting wood—it's recreation for him. At least, it's a change from his regular routine.

In spite of the adjustments she has had to make in Alaska, Yvonne said she liked living there.

"Alaska is a place for young people who want to get on their feet," she said. "It's a place to get to know yourself if you're young and tough and willing to work hard; it's a good place. You can be an individual—do your own thing, but you can't afford not to be somebody's friend. There just aren't

Yvonne Scott enjoys Alaska, but really is here to be with her husband.

that many people here."

I liked Yvonne and wished to know her better. I yearned to meet the natives and become involved in their world, too. What part could I play here? I'd had experience as teacher, journalist, photographer, waitress and recreation leader. I'd worked in a library and in a grocery store. I'd often thought I'd like to run a bookstore or be a librarian. Certainly there were opportunities for people in all of these vocations. But if I really wanted to do them, why couldn't I do it at home? Perhaps there may be more competition for these positions in Michigan, but persistence could win out. What was I really looking for?

Was I really willing to change my lifestyle or was I blinded by romantic imagination? I wanted to talk with someone else who had sorted it out. Kathy Cramer thought maybe Gretchen could help.

Alone together

"It's good to be a long way from those who are living the cowboy myth," said Gretchen Walker. Gretchen, who was David and Kathy Cramer's sometime babysitter, lived her own brand of life in a tiny, newly built cabin a short hike back into the forest along Alaska Highway 1, south of Tok. Her place was only three miles from Cramers—next door by Alaskan standards.

Gretchen was 35. Her long black hair hung down her back in a thick braid. Her plaid shirt and blue jeans affirmed that she belonged here. She came into the country, as they say, with her father when she was fresh out of high school and eager for adventure.

"My father was transferred here," Gretchen said, shifting her position as she sat cross-legged on the braided rug beside the wood stove. "He needed my company. I didn't get along with my mother, so I was happy to come along with Dad, but I didn't intend to remain in Alaska. I had planned to go back to college, but after awhile, you can't go back. You don't fit in.

"Dad taught me a lot about living, but he lost control of his own life. He had gone through a divorce just before we came up here. His life was all broken up. He was running away, but he couldn't run away from himself, so he soon went back Outside. I've never quite gotten around to leaving."

Gretchen said she wanted her own way of life and didn't want to be bothered with things like looking at other people's yards and garbage and she didn't want to chain her dog.

She found adventure quickly in the form of a short-lived marriage to a swashbuckling adventurer. "My husband was a wildlife photographer and guide," Gretchen related, "He was a macho type who wanted to be in charge of everything—and everyone—including me. I did what he told me for awhile—cooked in hunting camps, washed dishes and baked sourdough bread the way my father had taught me."

Finally, Gretchen apparently had enough, for she's critical of people who try to dominate the lives of others, especially religious fundamentalists in her home town in Idaho whom she remembered with bitterness. "They wanted to enforce their brand of morality on everyone else," she said.

"For instance, they ostracize divorced women who are trying to support themselves," she said. "You either do things their way or you leave. Here in Alaska if people don't like what you're doing, they'll leave you alone. Here you can do whatever you're capable of doing—work wise. Nobody will bat an eye if a woman wants to drive an earthmover."

I began to see that, contrary to what many people back home in the Lower 48 suspected, Alaska is not full of social misfits. People who run away from problems other places aren't going to last very long up here either if the problem they're trying to run away from is *themselves*.

Gretchen came *to* something. She didn't run *away* from anything.

Dave and I occupied the two simple wooden stools in the end of Gretchen's cabin that served as the kitchen, dining area and art studio. We studied several of the pretty young woman's whimsical landscape paintings as she continued to share her philosophy of life.

"I'm a vegetarian who likes seafood, so I can manage to live off the land and trade for food as well as for other goods," she explained. "For instance, my wood stove was a barter for one of my paintings and a sweater I had knitted."

Later at the Burnt Paw Gift shop in Tok we purchased one of Gretchen's drawings of a moose inked onto a fist-size tree fungus. The miniature drawing was done with skill and taste and it's one of the few souvenirs of our travels we've kept for ourselves.

Besides her artwork, Gretchen made warm outdoor clothing and camping equipment for herself and her nine-year-old daughter, Mary Ann.

Gretchen Walker

"New equipment is expensive," she said, "and secondhand parkas, pants and backpacks just aren't available up here because people literally wear them until they're no longer usable."

Asked whether she gardens, Gretchen said she'd rather spend her time hiking, canoeing and mountain climbing. She added that the greatest difficulty she has had to face isn't the lack of money. It's the physical separation from her mother and sisters back in Idaho that bothers her. She misses them a lot.

"People need a role model when rearing children" she said. "Parents can help. An extended family is important."

Mary Ann, a product of Gretchen's brief marriage, spent summers with her mother in the bush cabin and lived during the school year with her father in a more populated part of the Kenai Pennisula, off Alaska's southern coast. Gretchen passed the dark winter months alone in her cabin making crafts to sell during the next tourist season and doing some cross country skiing.

"There are advantages to being alone," she said. "When you're living with someone else, you can expect a lot of tension in relationships toward late winter. Stress hormones are high and cabin fever is rampant. February is more difficult the farther north you are.

"The good side is that it's nice to have two people to share the work in the winter. Two people can cut wood, drag logs

Gretchen and her daughter Mary Ann spend summers together.

and carry wood to the cabin together.

"But then spring is the time for break-up. Every March about ice break-up time, you see couples breaking up, too. They needed each other for support and survival during the winter, but when the first chance comes to get out, one of them goes. Usually it's the woman who leaves. More men seem to be able to live alone in the wilderness—but then here I am."

I wanted to spend more time with Gretchen. I admired a woman who could make it on her own—one who would take off and hike, canoe and backpack through life by herself.

I was glad that Dave and I share many of the same interests and as a result would do many things together. Yet, I also remembered the minister's quotation from Khahil Ghibran at our brief and simple wedding ceremony: "Let there be gaps in your togetherness."

Being independent and decisive is a state of mind, however, not a geographic location. Alaskan people helped re-emphasize this crucial point for me and this has since given me courage to go ahead and tackle more projects on my own, without waiting to see whether someone else would come along.

Five years later, we looked for Gretchen and found that she was no longer alone. She and Chris Janowsky had married and built a log cabin west of Tok. Gretchen, again with long black braids, and wearing a tan T-shirt with a sled dog silkscreened on it, was cooking salmon for lunch. She said that Mary Ann, now 14, had chosen to remain with her father year round now because "life is easier there."

Moose antlers hung on the rough exterior of Gretchen's studio. Sockeye salmon filets were drying on racks in the smokehouse. Alderwood was providing the smoke for the week's catch from their fishwheel. A waterfall, wishing well and pagoda in the yard revealed traces of Eastern influence. The calla lilies were about to bloom and an arrangement of "Flight of the Condor" was on the stereo the day we visited the cabin. The flutelike music lent an air of mystery to the scene.

"I met Chris at an Emergency Medical Technician class here in Tok," Gretchen explained. "We've been together three years. We got married to be together. If people want to be apart they shouldn't be married. Chris and I work well together. It's good to have a partner who's headed in the same direction as you are."

Chris used to be a plumber and has been a martial arts instructor. He and Gretchen sometimes teach survival skills. Gretchen said she'd like to sell oil paintings but didn't feel like going to the *right* parties and hobnobbing with gallery owners. So she continued to market her fungus paintings which she said were selling well.

But when it's fishing time, Gretchen and Chris go fishing. They smoke their salmon at a low temperature and then raise the temperature to cook it. Then they pickle and can it.

Gretchen continues to be an individual when it comes to a philosophy of life. She's concerned about government invasion of privacy and the fact that people are so busy earning money that they fail to enjoy their children. She's also concerned that people lose their individuality when following the crowd.

"You have to fit in and dress the right way," she said. "You become a cog in a machine. People choose to live in the bush for personal freedom and integrity. Too many people are overworked neurotics who come home to watch TV."

I appreciated what Gretchen was saying, but it set me to thinking. And I began to play the devil's advocate. The TV problem could be anywhere—Alaska or back Outside, I thought. And people could be themselves anywhere, too. They didn't really have to live in the bush, did they?

The Farm

What do you do with a 70-pound cabbage? I asked 73-year-old Max Sherrod.

"Take it to the fair!" replied Max who is known throughout Alaska for the prize-winning vegetables he exhibited proudly at the state fair each autumn for half a century.

Max and his wife Dorothy made the long journey in 1935 from southern Michigan to help open up for farming the now productive Matanuska Valley in south-central Alaska.

For this couple, true twentieth century pioneers, Alaska has been their life for more than 50 years.

"You must visit Max and Dorothy," our friend Berenice Lowe from Battle Creek had told us as she jotted down the couple's address and telephone number.

So after leaving Tok, we headed to the agricultural center at the town of Palmer, site of the Alaska state fair, forty miles northeast of Anchorage. We stopped at the gift shop which we'd been told was one of the best for buying Alaskan souvenirs. After choosing a few things for our children I went to the telephone.

Dorothy answered and urged, "Yes, come on out. We have a Grange meeting to go to tonight, but that isn't until 6:30." I assured her that we would be gone long before six as it was only three o'clock then. She gave us directions and we drove out to their country home which claimed a spectacular view.

By the time we arrived—about fifteen minutes later—Dorothy had made some decisions. We were to attend the Grange supper meeting with them and we were to spend the night in their guest room.

We protested that we could sleep in our pickup, but Dorothy had made up her mind. "That's no place to sleep in the rain." (Yes, it was raining again.) "You can stay with us. Lots of folks have been nice to us through the years. We can't repay them, but we can help somebody else."

Who could argue with a philosophy like that? So we accepted their gracious invitation and enjoyed the potluck, conversation and program at the Grange where we met several key figures in Alaskan agriculture.

Later that evening we heard Max and Dorothy's story. They were real pioneers and participated in the beginnings of agriculture in Alaska's fertile Matanuska Valley. But first, Max insisted on telling us about his giant vegetables.

The growing season lasts only a few short weeks, but since the summer sun shines nearly 24 hours a day, 70-pound cabbages, 30-pound turnips and baseball-size radishes are not unusual in this pest-free arctic Garden of Eden.

Throughout his career on the Alaskan frontier, Max Sherrod has been recognized as an ace vegetable grower. He and Dorothy made a good living from truck farming and enjoyed competing for record produce. Among his accomplishments, Max has produced a world record cabbage weighing 72 pounds, a 50-pound turnip and a 16-pound sweet potato.

A famous postcard, still on sale in Alaskan souvenir shops, shows a trick photo of a moose dwarfed by Max's gigantic prize cabbage. Actually, the moose on the postcard is a

Max Sherrod continues to grow vegetables in his retirement years.

miniature toy, but the caption doesn't tell you that. Even so, this was one huge cabbage!

Max and Dorothy had met as nursing students in Battle Creek, Michigan. After graduating, marrying and practicing nursing in the community for a time, they began to feel there was no future for them there during the Great Depression.

"I was earning $100 a month at the hospital and saw no chance for advancement," Max said. "I was restless so we set out for Seattle and bought tickets for Alaska."

"Max had to persuade me to come," Dorothy admitted. "My mother thought she'd never see me again if I took off for Alaska. I did go back to visit, but I never considered going back to the Midwest to live."

As they traveled west, Max and Dorothy dreamed of following their star north to "opportunity." That same summer two hundred other farm families from Michigan, Wisconsin and Minnesota were also making the trek from the "Lower 48," the term used by Alaskans to describe the 48 states in the main body of the United States.

The depression of the 1930's had forced many to pull up stakes at home and reach for new land where they could afford to put down roots. The opportunity was offered to these new settlers by President Franklin D. Roosevelt, as part of the Federal Emergency Relief Act. Roosevelt billed this legislation as a relief program for the unemployed, a stimulant to population growth in Alaska and a demonstration of the territory's agricultural potential.

Each family was to be given 80 acres of Alaskan land, a horse, a well, a barn, some tools and up to $285 worth of furniture.

Some of the colonists setting out by steamer from Seattle became ill and needed nursing care. When federal officials in charge of the program discovered that Max and Dorothy had civil service papers and were nurses as well, they made them an offer.

"The government offered to pay our travel fare if we'd care for the families that were ill," Max said. "So we actually worked for our passage to Alaska."

"Since our transportation was being paid for, we cashed in our tickets and bought additional tools and supplies we thought we'd need in Alaska," Dorothy added.

Getting started in an underdeveloped land wasn't easy. The Sherrods had a rough beginning in their new home, but they met challenges as they came up.

"We finally arrived by bus in Palmer, Alaska, at 6:30 p. m. on May 28, 1935," Max remembered. "The stuff we'd sent ahead of us hadn't yet arrived."

Neither were any homes awaiting them; everyone was starting from scratch. But there were friendly people in Palmer, including the resident Catholic priest. "He moved out of his 12 x 14-foot tent so we with our young daughter and another couple with three kids could move into it," Max said.

Then, without wasting a moment, Max got busy planting a vegetable garden. "I had seeds in the ground within three days after we arrived. That way I knew we'd have something to eat that winter," he said.

Max also proceeded to build a 16 by 20-foot wooden frame and cover it with canvas to serve as the family's home during that first Alaskan winter.

"We had hoped to homestead in Palmer," Max said. "But by the time we arrived, the government had either withdrawn the land or it had already been taken."

Since the Sherrods had no car, they had to live in town. Max recalls they used to get around on bicyles.

Faced with the propect of remaining for some time in the village of Palmer, Max took a job first in a warehouse, then in a local chicken hatchery. "I had worked for a poultryman for room and board years before in Michigan. There was such a tremendous demand for fresh eggs in Alaska that a hatchery was an important business," he said.

Max's hard work and management skills soon earned him a promotion to manager of the hatchery at what was a good salary for that time—$175 a month. "Here was a 25,000 egg incubator and I made it work," he said.

But soon Max's nursing skills were needed again. The local hospital drafted him because of disease epidemics sweeping the area. "Measles, mumps, scarlet fever and chicken pox kept us busy," he said. "Then when three men in Palmer came down with smallpox, I moved in with them and nursed them. We were quarantined for 24 days."

Max remembers his early nursing days in Alaska as times when he had to work under pretty extreme circumstances. "We had no modern medications and our training hadn't included some of the things we were called on to do.

"But on the frontier there was no one else to do the work. There were no interns available and the nearest doctor was miles away. We delivered babies, took x-rays and administered anesthetics."

Frontier medicine was challenging, but by 1938 Max was restless again. "I got tired of nursing," he said. "I kept thinking of the good old days on the farm, walking behind the horses, so I began buying land.

"Our first farm consisted of about 15 acres and we paid $1.25 an acre for the undeveloped ground about 40 miles from Anchorage. We had to bulldoze trees and build a half-mile road to the place."

Those years were tough times for Alaskans. Max recalls the winter of 1937-38 when there was no food coming in from Outside because of a longshoremen's strike. The dense spruce forests were poor habitat for wild game, and hard-pressed farmers even killed off valuable breeding hogs because meat was so scarce.

But as the human population in the area increased, so did the wildlife. "As we cleared the land," Max said, "young brush grew up—tender willow that attracted moose."

By 1940 Max and Dorothy were finally able to move from town to their farm. Because the Rural Electric Administration lines didn't come into the Sherrods' area until 1942, the couple had to generate their own electricity. "I installed a diesel powered generating plant," Max said, "and then we had lights and power to pump the water, too."

As Max spoke of the arrival of electricity to his farm, I recalled it had been about 1940 that the electric lines had arrived in the rural area of Ashley in central Michigan where I grew up. I remembered how exciting it was to have electric light switches to turn on and off instead of lighting the kerosene lamps.

Farmers faced an enormous challenge on the Alaskan frontier, but the Sherrods kept at it and discovered the virtues of the Matanuska Valley. "If you have a south slope," Max explained, "you have warmer weather and you can grow vegetables faster. The soil here is black and takes in the heat readily.

"Insect pests that destroy crops in the Lower 48 are practically nonexistent here, so we don't have to use pesticides. I think Alaska is the best place in the world to grow vegetables."

When world War II swelled the population of Anchorage with GIs and civilian war workers, there was such a tremendous market for fresh, local vegetables that the Sherrods and others couldn't grow enough to meet the demand.

"We supplied a lot of food—especially to the military," Max said. "We would have to bid competitively to get that business. Then Dorothy would drive the truck to Anchorage with produce for the Army base and other customers."

Max's job during the war was to keep the farm producing. "Military personnel would come up here on leave from Anchorage to work in the potato fields," he said.

By 1948 there were only 50 farms remaining in the colony as smaller plots of ground were absorbed by larger agricultural operators and more families gave up farming to work for wages.

But the Sherrods' operation continued to expand. They not only grew and wholesaled vegetables, they operated two farm markets for fourteen years. Again this venture was spawned from Max's previous experiences in Michigan.

As a boy, Max had sold peaches, grapes and apples from the family car parked along the highway on Sunday afternoons. Max recalled, "We also had a vegetable route in southwestern Michigan that we covered twice a week, selling to Chicago people vacationing in the area."

Eventually Dorothy and Max owned 146 Alaskan acres, 70 of which they cultivated. Now they've sold off most of their land and are retired, living in a spot with green meadows framed by snowcapped mountains. Their daughter Janet lives nearby, and Max and Dorothy proudly show visitors snapshots of their four grandchildren and several great-grandchildren.

Max continues to grow potatoes, beans and strawberries in a small garden. He also raises tomatoes, cucumbers and corn in his small greenhouse. "You can't grow tomatoes and corn outdoors in Alaska," he explains. "The nights are too cold."

Like many other successful Alaskans, the Sherrods now enjoy the winter months in Hawaii. Max spends his summers gardening in Alaska and his winters gardening on the grounds of their new home on the Big Island of Hawaii.

Max has also traveled to Scandinavia, Australia, New Zealand and The Soviet Union—always looking for potato farmers with whom to exchange information about farming.

As we heard the Sherrods' story, we felt privileged to be

Max and Dorothy Sherrod share many memories of their early days in the Matanuska Valley

visiting with them in their home. We learned they've had such prestigious visitors as Thomas E. Dewey, the 1948 Republican presidential candidate; Sir Edmund Hillary, conqueror of Mount Everest; Jim Whittaker, first North American to climb Mount Everest; and Will Rogers and his pilot Wiley Post, who landed in Palmer just before their ill-fated 1935 flight beyond the Arctic Circle.

It was early July when we visited the Sherrods, and the cabbages weren't yet mature; but Max and Dorothy loaded us down with early carrots and lettuce which we ate as we traveled. The vegetables were not only delicious, but they reminded us of the friendliness of Alaskans.

We visited the Sherrods in their winter home in Hawaii in January, 1986. They had recently constructed this home and planned to sell it and build another. Projects like these keep Max, now nearly 80 years old, alive.

In July 1986 we visited them again in Palmer and helped Max celebrate his birthday on the Fourth of July. Relatives and neighbors arrived carrying food, presents and flowers. We spent much of the day eating as we visited. Before the day was over, I discovered to my chagrin that I'd eaten five desserts. Certainly no way to keep one's weight reasonable. But there had been three birthday cakes, one of them a cheese cake, plus a cherry cobbler and some fabulous brownies. What could one do but eat them?

Matanuska Valley potatoes

At Max Sherrod's party we met Max and Dorothy's daughter Janet, their son-in-law, three grandchildren and eight great-grandchildren as well as numerous friends and neighbors. One couple was Ben and Suus VanderWeele who had immigrated to Alaska from Holland in 1968 and purchased Sherrods' vegetable stand and twenty acres of land.

Ben had wanted to be a farmer, but there was little opportunity at that time in the Netherlands because of the extremely high cost of the small amount of land available.

"My parents' farm was condemned by city expansion," Ben told us. "Our friends who have remained in Holland have had to work hard there. It's crowded with too many people. There are more farmers than land to cultivate."

Ben and Suus wanted to find a frontier. Ben corresponded at length with Max, learning from him about the Matanuska Valley, its soil, people, crops, climate and way of life.

Eventually after Max and Dorothy visited Ben in Holland, they decided to act as Ben's official sponsors. After months of government red tape, Ben and Suus were permitted to settle in Alaska because they were purchasing Sherrods' established roadside market business. Max helped them become adjusted to Alaskan soil and oriented them in the ways of vegetable growing in the Matanuska Valley.

Now, Ben and Suus have expanded their holdings to 90 acres just outside Palmer where they raise potatoes, lettuce,

Ben and Suus Vander Weele experiment with a variety of methods for growing vegetables.

cabbage and carrots for sale primarily to military bases and to chain retail stores in Anchorage and Fairbanks.

A dozen or more employees are involved in production and packaging. VanderWeeles sell their carrots on the fresh market in September, October and November; and although potatoes are harvested in September, they store much of their crop in an enormous insulated warehouse until market demand is greater between January and July.

Ninety-eight percent of their potatoes go to the fresh market; however, they supply a few to a mini processing plant that produces ready-to-heat hash browns and diced potatoes for restaurants.

"The big challenge of potatoes is the marketing," Ben said. "I like to have an assured market before I plant. It would be very easy to overproduce."

But Ben says it's difficult to get a written commitment from buyers. He said that a couple of large stores, a couple of small ones and a few wholesalers handle the volume of produce in Alaska. Roadside stands and individuals sell a relatively small share.

"Limited population here is a problem. There are only so many people to eat the produce. When lettuce is ready to harvest, it has to be sold. Quality is gone within three days. Potatoes, on the other hand, can be kept for eleven months if necessary.

"When we came from Holland 18 years ago, we grew produce for the roadside market," Ben said. "Rhubarb and radishes were first in the spring, and we continued to sell fresh vegetables and fruits throughout the summer." Suus ran the roadside market for fourteen years.

"We had cash every day then from June to September," she recalls. "Now we have to wait 60 days or more for our checks. The roadside market was a good deal then; but we closed it four years ago because the supermarket chains are too competitive and customers want a complete line of produce. Fifty percent of the people who visited our roadside market stopped to purchase items we didn't raise ourselves, and we had to pay more for peaches and grapes wholesale than retailers in town were selling them for.

"Supermarkets can offer year round produce—grapes from Chile, apples from New Zealand, etc." Suus added. "This started happening about ten years ago when they began building the pipeline here in Alaska."

"Yet, as more people arrived, more and better services arrived and our standard of living improved," Ben added. Ben certainly isn't against progress. He has conducted experiments to try to increase quality and yield, and he produces all of the potato seed for their plantings, buying test tube tubers from Cornell University.

The VanderWeeles were also the first in Alaska to install a vacuum cooler for their lettuce—about four years ago—and they also experiment with irrigation. They have plans now for a new refrigeration room in a corner of the 266 x 100-foot storage building they recently constructed for themselves.

"We pay as we go," Ben said. "I don't like to work for a bank." In keeping with this philosophy, Ben sometimes buys used equipment instead of new.

Despite the problems he faces, Ben feels he made the right decision to immigrate to the northern frontier. "Our quality of life is better here than it would have been had we remained in Holland," he said. "Alaska is a good environment in which to live. It's a good place to raise a family. That part is more rewarding than anything else."

Dairying with faith and frugality

A decision to put her name into an Alaskan land lottery changed the course of Pat Schenk's life. The girl who grew up in rural Michigan suddenly found herself co-owner of a dairy farm near Delta Junction in the Alaskan interior.

While we were in Palmer, I had visited the Cooperative Extension Service office and asked personnel there for names of farmers who might be good subjects for interviews. One of the extension agents suggested Pat and Neil Schenk.

A few days later, I phoned the Schenks from Fairbanks and they agreed to talk with us that same evening. It would be nearly nine o'clock before we could arrive, but that didn't bother the Schenks. It was summer and there would be daylight nearly all night.

Pat and Neil have lived in Alaska since 1970. Neil had been in the construction business and Pat occupied herself with numerous hobbies. Until recently, the Schenks lived near Denali National Park in an A-frame cabin Neil had built.

"I didn't want to move," Pat said. "I liked living in the bush. True, we had no phone. We had electricity and running water only when we used our generator. I loved the snow—even when we had to dig down through the snow to the woodpile." (The snow was sometimes six feet deep.)

"We had to snowmobile in the last four miles to our cabin; I taught the kids their schooling by correspondence. In doing so, I really learned to appreciate teachers."

But when through the state lottery in January 1980 Pat won the right to buy 80 acres in Alaska, it meant moving to Delta Junction. By state law, lottery winners had to live on the land and farm it if they were to accept the privilege of purchasing the land.

Neil had grown up on a Michigan dairy farm so dairying was a natural operation to consider. After purchasing the 80 lottery acres for $100 an acre, Pat and Neil bought several hundred more acres from private owners and rented another 700. Then they were farming 1,200 acres and milking 45 cows.

"We're the largest dairy in the area," Neil said. "Actually there are only thirteen or fourteen dairies in the entire state."

In March 1980 they moved with their 15-year-old daughter Kim and 12-year-old son Neil to the newly acquired property. "We lived in a 12 x 16-foot shed with a bunk area for the kids until we could get a mobile home moved in," Pat recalled.

Pat and Neil Schenk operate a dairy farm near Delta Junction.

At the time Dave and I visited them, Neil was making plans to put a basement under the mobile unit.

The couple have been amused by questions asked by friends and relatives Outside. Some people seem to think that Alaska is a land of ice and snow with igloos everywhere.

"How do you live in Alaska?" they've been asked by their friends in Michigan.

"We live just like you do," Pat tells them. "We eat, sleep, work, buy groceries, get together with friends."

Even though igloos are nonexistent except for some temporary winter homes on the ice built by Eskimo hunters, there are some things unique about living in Alaska. For one thing, Neil delivers the milk to the dairy himself. "We're lucky it's only three miles away," he remarks.

"The cost of living is about 25 percent higher in Alaska than in most places in the Lower 48," Pat explained. "We buy our groceries by the case in Fairbanks. I freeze and can a great deal of food, but still we spend about $75 a week locally for groceries."

"I guess what I miss most from Michigan are sweet corn and watermelons," she said. "I paid $10 for a watermelon to celebrate the Fourth of July. I told the kids that was our melon for the season." Pat has a big garden and a small greenhouse for tomatoes and sweet corn.

Like most individuals who survive in Alaska, the Schenks

have learned to adapt—to the weather, to the daylight hours (or lack of them) and to the system of bartering. Pat keeps a flock of 15 laying hens and buys baby chicks regularly to ensure they'll have fresh eggs. She barters with the neighbors when she has a surplus of eggs.

"Sometimes 30 calves might be born in a single month," Pat said. "I might have 30 calves a day to feed, and in winter we can't get rid of the bull calves. The nearest slaughter house is 120 miles away and it costs too much to raise the bull calves. We've even given some away."

Pat said she had talked with a native Alaskan neighbor lady who told her that Holstein cow skin would make nice mukluks (Eskimo boots). Pat has considered exchanging some hides for a new pair of mukluks.

Neil was hoping that in a few years the farm operation would grow enough so they could hire some help. "Pat and I can't even go to town together unless we're home by 4 p. m." he said. "We need dairy help, but we can't find workers. Some people can't stand Alaska because it's too cold. Some get homesick. Others just haven't had farming experience."

So Pat and Neil do more of the work themselves than they would choose and accept the fact that for a few years, they may be tied to the farm.

"Summers are great," Pat says, "but we enjoy our time together as a family in the winter. We read together, play games and work puzzles. We don't have time for cabin fever. We're too busy working on projects.

"One day I wanted a new leather belt but couldn't find one I liked," Pat said, "so I asked a friend if she would tool one for me."

"Tool your own," the friend told her. So Pat did, and soon she was making and selling belts.

Later when Pat wanted a painted fungus, Neil told her, "If you want one, paint one." Soon she was selling painted fungi as well as belts and other arts and crafts at the gift shop in the visitors' center in Palmer. She took up crocheting, knitting, rug hooking, macrame and acrylic and pastel painting. When she isn't working on crafts, she's reading books about the history of Alaska.

Other Alaskans use the wintertime to play cards, square dance, cross country and downhill ski, and to race teams of dogs. Then there are snowmobiling, trapping, ice fishing, wood cutting and pool tournaments.

We were told about a fellow who reportedly goes to the bother of starting his automobile in the winter just to drive into town and brag about how easily the vehicle started at 50 degrees below zero.

Pat and Neil will probably remain in Alaska, I thought. They're hooked on the beauty of the state. The snowcapped peaks of the Alaska Range provide a spectacular view for residents of the valley. Neil puts his feelings succinctly. "After you've lived where there are mountains, it's hard to go where they aren't," he said.

After traveling through the Alaska Range by the light of the Midnight Sun, we knew what Neil meant. After completing our interview with Schenks that evening about midnight, we drove back to Fairbanks through nearly 100 miles of orange and gold continuous twilight.

We watched the sun set and rise again all within a couple of hours. Here was some of the most beautiful scenery in the world—with colors of sunset and sunrise blending in together.

That was one of two nights that we stayed up all night while we were in Alaska. Neither Dave nor I are night owls and so this was an occasion. We were both too tired to photograph the spectacular view, but the indescribable beauty is etched in my memory forever.

Returning to visit the Schenks five years later, we found they had been through some rough financial times. "Pat and I began storming at each other," Neil said. "Suddenly we realized that our marriage was in danger. We began looking at possibilities. We never thought we'd split up, but stress was getting to us. But we knew we wanted to save our marriage."

"People can get so emotional that they don't evaluate things," Pat said. "You feel like you have to yell at somebody, and we were yelling at each other.

"We'd been through similar problems before and we were almost divorced eleven years ago," Pat said. "We recognized that many of our problems then were due to stress and we had worked through them. We decided we could do it again. We remembered that we like each other for the same reasons we did when we were first married. We're the same persons."

The conscientious couple had been working through their personal problems even though financial troubles continued to plague them.

"The milk processing plant burned down and we had to ship milk to Anchorage," Neil explained. "At one time we were dumping milk for several months and we culled our milk cows down to twenty. Now we're back to milking fifty cows and the processing plant is back in business. There just isn't enough milk in Alaska, but we can expand our operation only as we get the money."

One possible source of income would be for Schenks to raise barley, but Neil says they're handicapped by the fact that there's no slaughterhouse in Alaska now. "With no slaughterhouse, there are no animals to eat the grain we might raise," he said.

"Yet things are getting better and at this rate, we can pay off our loan in thirty years."

"I think our Christian background has helped us," Pat said. "We believe in prayer and it has worked for us. We want to remain in Alaska. We've lived in Kenai, Palmer and Denali. I never thought I would like the Interior, but now we find we like the Interior best.

"We like it here," Pat repeated. "We'd rather be here than anywhere else."

Where the grass grows greener

Because I've written articles for *Michigan Farmer* magazine since 1969, I'm always looking for stories about farm families. In an effort to learn more about Alaskan agriculture, we drove to Delta Junction, suggested in *The Milepost* as the place to look for barley farmers.

Byron and Ileen Hollembaek and their two sons are modern day pioneers who make a good living from growing and exporting hardy varieties of grass and barley seed. They also run an Angus-Chianiana cow-calf beef operation,

It had taken 81 semi loads to move their belongings and equipment from Palmer, where they had farmed for 30 years, to virgin land near Delta Junction. "We cleared trees, raked the land with a root rake, piled and raked the stumps using equipment seldom familiar to farmers outside Alaska," Byron explained. "We logged four million board feet of lumber, but it's difficult to sell it here because people can buy lumber cheaper in Canada.

"We drew lots for 22 tracts of land in the Delta Barley Project," Byron added. "Our name wasn't drawn, so we bought 914 acres from a person from Oregon who did win, but decided not to farm."

The Hollembaeks said they find it's easier to farm at Delta Junction than in Palmer because crops ripen faster.

"Most of what we produce is sold to the Orient and in the lower 48 states," Byron said. "We've been shipping grass seed to Japan since 1981 and we can't meet the demand. We have to level more land and get the wild grasses and weeds out before we can grow more seed." Byron owns greenhouses in Oregon and New Mexico where seed samples are grown and thus they can get test results of the seed more quickly than if they wait a year for the Alaska growing season.

Hollembaeks were selling seed to a couple of their neighbors who, in turn, became seed suppliers; however the neighbors were going to require combines of their own so they could harvest the seed at peak time.

"We have nearly three million dollars invested in machinery," Byron said, "and barley is selling for only $83 to $89 a ton in Seattle. We have to increase our barley acreage to make any money. Some of us could raise hay, for there are horses scattered all over the state who could eat the hay; but we can't afford to deliver it."

Ileen's contribution to the farm operation is to sell seeds and handwork and to help with farm tours. "Visitors come by

Ileen and Byron Hollembaek have been farming for thirty years.

the bus load, including paid tour groups and children from area schools," Ileen said. "The kids like to come and dig in the dirt and chase rabbits."

Although school buses bring groups on field trips, it's more difficult to get the buses to pick up the grandchildren who live on the farm and to take them to classes every day.

"The bus will come only if there are at least three children on a particular road," Ileen said. "We live six miles from our mail box."

So the children have to be driven to meet the school bus.

But the journey can combine nature and art lessons as a family of foxes romps among fields of flaming magenta fireweed and golden rapeseed blossoms.

Hollembaeks had recently completed a huge structure with living quarters at one end for two families. Byron and Ileen and their son Eric live in the three-bedroom apartment on the first floor. Their son Scott and his wife and their four children live upstairs in a four bedroom apartment. Solar collector panels cover the south side of the roof and an insulated collection tank for hot water is located beside the house. The long building also contains a shop, seed drying room, office and storage rooms. We were reminded of old European buildings which included both house and barn under one roof.

Back in Delta Junction, I asked extension agent Don Quarberg to explain the Hollembaeks' success.

"Hollembaek has been farming in Alaska for 30 years," Don said, "and he has established marketing opportunities of his own."

Again I was reminded of the importance of marketing. It doesn't matter how much you produce or how great the quality is. If you can't sell it, you can't make a profit.

The City

"I didn't come to Alaska to hunt, to fish or to live in a log cabin," Bob Ely emphasized. "The challenge for me was to build a law firm, to create an institution, to pave the wilderness, to try to make Anchorage into a Detroit."

I didn't think I could agree with that last objective, but we had come to listen, not to criticize.

Bob, a prominent attorney in Anchorage, graciously agreed to spend an afternoon with us. As we drank iced tea on the veranda of his comfortable home, secluded by trees from the otherwise quite densely populated street, we learned Bob had grown up in New England and attended both Yale and Harvard.

"Statehood for Alaska was being discussed in the legislature between my second and third year of law school," Bob recalled.

Hearing Bob speak about statehood brought back memories. I'd grown up pledging allegiance to a flag with 48 stars. Hawaii and Alaska had been added in 1959.

Bob continued, "I was a freshman counselor at the university, and one of my freshmen was the son of an Alaskan banker. When I met the banker, he encouraged me to come to Alaska.

"It was a great place to be. I'd been a western history major. I'd never been West so I decided to go as far west as I could. This decision delighted my father, horrified my mother and astonished my friends. That was in '59.

"I became a law clerk for a federal judge which was a prestigious thing to do. It was great to be here during the transition of Alaska from a territory to a state.The selection of judges was an exciting time. I was here as the whole judicial system was being established.

"Eventually, three of us decided to found a commercial corporate law firm—like other large cities had," Bob explained.

"It was a romantic new frontier kind-of-thing. Later I worked for a year and a half in Washington, D. C. There I met the girl who became my wife, then I returned to the same firm in Anchorage. Our firm has grown so that now we have offices in Anchorage, Juneau and Washington, D. C."

Bob talked about the question of Willow as a prospective capital for Alaska. Willow has been rejected by Alaskan voters as the site of the capital, but at the time we talked with Bob, it was still a real possibility.

Willow, 69 miles north of Anchorage and 289 miles south of Fairbanks, listed 576 residents in the 1980 census, but the area population had been growing rapidly since the region was designated as a possible site for the new Alaska state capitol. Some politicans and businessmen in both Fairbanks and Anchorage wanted the capitol in their own city. Willow had been viewed as a compromise.

"No, I'm not interested in developing Willow," Bob said that day we talked with him. "But there are challenges everywhere. Anchorage is cosmopolitan, an international mix of people and occupations. There are fisheries, the military, the oil, the miners. Most everyone came from somewhere else.

They're here because they had the nerve to make an affirmative decision to come here and continually make the decision to remain.

"Although Anchorage is a cosmopolitan city, other parts of Alaska are quite provincial," Bob explained. Kids are afraid to go away from Alaska to school or to work unless they've traveled extensively with their parents. This was just one of the many paradoxes we found about The Great Land.

"Of course, there have been difficulties here," Bob said. "I miss the extended family, a family we can visit, where the kids can stay in touch with their grandparents. It costs many dollars to visit the grandparents or even to exchange information via telephone."

Bob and his wife had three children—a 13-year-old boy, 11-year-old girl and 7-year-old boy. He explained that they're faced with a new dilemma now. He said. "The challenge here has been seeing the town grow and contributing a service to the city. Now that the challenge is gone, it's no longer satisfying here. I want a change, but here are the three kids coming up—they'll need to be put through college. My parents put me through college. I want to do the same for my children."

Bob has a secure position in Anchorage. If he remains, he'll be able to send the children to the college of their choice. If he goes in search of new opportunitiies, there will be risks. The financial ones concerned him most at the time we talked.

We thought it ironic that we were talking with someone who had been in Alaska for more than 20 years but who had now decided he needed some greater challenge. We weren't sure that Bob would remain in Alaska. He might indeed seek opportunities elsewhere. Had he been a politican, he might be running for governor or attorney general. Was that what he had wanted? We wondered what Bob was looking for, but we hadn't been quick enough to ask. Bob had certainly been successful in Alaska. But successful by whose definition? As I pondered this, I realized again, "It's all relative."

From courtroom to drilling rig

"My dream of being a lawyer had turned from sugar to shit. The stress was too much. I could feel ulcers and cardiac problems coming. I was drinking too much."

That was Jim Rhoads speaking, former Anchorage senior juvenile court judge. On this particular morning Dave and I sat with Jim and his wife Cheryl in an out of the way suburban restaurant where we would be able to talk uninterrupted. We had met Cheryl the summer before at a luncheon with several Anchorage Press Women.

I had been impressed with Cheryl's businesslike yet warm and friendly manner and we were delighted when she and her husband agreed to meet us and tell their story. Jim is a tall, dark, muscular fellow who began spilling his tale immediately. Actually the session seemed to be therapeutic for Jim, Cheryl confided to me as we left the restaurant.

Over a breakfast of bacon and eggs, Jim began by describing how they'd chosen the mountainside site for their beautiful home named "Cloud Dance" overlooking Anchorage just outside the boundary of Chugach State Park.

"We researched the area and read geological surveys to determine how to set the house to best weather the storms," Jim explained. "We designed our home to survive nature. It has five roof lines designed to break up the wind."

The conversation soon shifted to their roots and how the couple met. Cheryl grew up on Long Island and attended the University of Nevada in Las Vegas where she majored in French. Jim's roots were in Oregon and Washington state with the out-of-doors at his finger tips. He was a political science major at the University.

"Jim and I met in French class in 1964 when he was just recovering from a divorce," Cheryl said. "I tutored him at no charge although I was charging others $3 an hour. I'd had six years of French before that and my goal was to get my Ph.D and become an interpreter at the United Nations.

"I'd been a good student, but I couldn't continue a high class New York lifestyle in Nevada. I failed a major class in the second semester of college and drew a mental block in French. Suddenly I couldn't speak the language after six years of study.

"My family didn't approve of Jim because he wasn't Jewish." However, Cheryl married Jim and left her Jewish family behind. She continued, "We went to Phoenix, Arizona where Jim went to school and interned as a family court judge. We had planned to settle in Phoenix, but decided there were too many people."

So the couple drove a VW bus to Alaska for a month's vacation.

"But after four days, we decided to move here," Cheryl said. "I think we knew before we left home that we would stay, for we had stored our belongings in a friend's garage. We called home and said, 'Send the kids and cats.' The three children and four cats arrived. We declared ourselves Alaskans and told everybody to shut the gates and not let anyone else in."

That attitude was one we'd heard before. Many people had found what they wanted in Alaska, and then realized the state would no longer be the same if the population increased. They could lose the lifestyle for which they came.

I recalled having covered a village meeting in mid-Michigan as a reporter. Approximately 100 citizens had gathered to protest the local road commission's plan to widen the main street.

"This was a good town to live in," the chairman of the meeting said. "Now that so many of you thought this would be a good place to live and moved here, we need to widen the road."

The citizens protested and to this day the road still hasn't been widened.

At any rate, Jim did trustee court work in Anchorage and

soon became the senior juvenile court judge.

"They told me I had a brilliant political career in my future," Jim said. "But I quit the job because of politics. State courts were putting in too many restrictions. I went into private law practice as a corporation attorney. In 1977 and 1978 bankruptcies doubled. Small and personal businesses were collapsing. I lost $40,000 the last year I practiced."

As he continued, I could sense the pain and conflict Jim had endured. "I realize I had become disenchanted with the hypocrisy. The judicial process of the law and its contradictions was too expensive. We don't provide the services people need.

"When I seriously considered politics, I decided I'd have to sell too much of myself to attain a political office. It's always a compromise. In Nevada, they'd been grooming me for the governorship. The political process is more accessible here in Alaska, but it's still the same process.

"Well, anyway," Jim continued, "I left the law firm and considered going into middle management. I thought my analytical mind, which is what attorneys have, is something a company could use. But there were no takers.

"At one point I was ready to manage a fishery but that didn't work out because there was a fishermen's strike that year.

"Now there were no takers for me—this brilliant attorney," Jim lamented. "My ego was deflated. I began looking for a job. I'd look for work and then go to the golf course and later come home having drunk a lot en route."

I could sympathize. Changing jobs is agonizing, but being between jobs is even more painful. I recalled having quit a teaching job that was driving me up the wall. I didn't want to be a quitter, but the stress was just too much. I found it especially difficult to leave a profession that I had prepared for in college and had planned to remain in until retirement.

Jim continued. "Finally I talked with a fellow with one of the oil companies. I told him I was hungry and needed to work. He told me that laborers on drilling crews (called roustabouts) were earning $67,000 a year.

"Six weeks later I had a job as a roustabout. I loved it. I had worked as a kid in a lumber camp. That had been heavy work and I'd driven a truck. I'd also been active in sports, but it had been 20 years since I'd done any real physical labor.

"That first year on the Slope darn near killed me. My shoulders and arms were numb for eight months and I developed tendonitis. I put on muscle, however, and as I worked with kids 20 years younger than I, they nicknamed me 'the Judge.' I worked for Parker Drilling who contracted with ARCO at drill site 14. We'd drill a hole down to 11,000 feet in 21 days.

"I went from a roustabout to a gopher to a roughneck. This was dangerous, dirty, hard, cold work. Often the chill factor was off the chart.

"I was nearly killed on the floor of the drilling site. I've broken ribs, separated shoulders and received many bruises. Once I hit the cradle (the framework supporting the equipment). If the cradle hadn't been there, I'd have been dead.

"Now I'm a mudmaker on the rig floor—a pit watcher who makes the mud. ('Mud' is a solution pumped into a well hole to lubricate the drilling tools.) I have to lift heavy sacks and watch the mud for signs of kick and keep the machinery working. But sometimes there are bonuses like finding wood that had been 2,000 feet underground—frozen wood with four-inch branches on it—from millions of years ago."

Jim said he enjoyed the physical labor and the lack of emotional stress on this job. "I'm still working towards a goal of middle management, but I may have to become a driller before I can advance to that point.

"The qualities you need to work on the North Slope are eye and motion coordination and adroitness. The stress level is different because you're accomplishing something physical. Here I work one week and have one week off."

While there are advantages to having whole blocks of time

off, I suspected that would be quite stressful for the spouse. Imagine doing your own thing all week and the next week having a husband in the house who either wants to be fed and entertained or to be left alone. Either way would require some adjustment. I thought if I were the spouse I'd want to be sure to have an away-from-home job myself.

And if I were the person working a week on and week off job, that would take some adjustment. I remembered the summer when I was 18 years old and was working the night shift waiting on tables in a restaurant. I never did figure out whether I slept six, seven or eight times a week. On my days off I didn't know when to sleep.

Cheryl, however, kept busy when Jim was working. Soon after they moved to Alaska, she answered a newspaper ad and landed a secretarial job in the public relations department of Aleyeska Pipeline Company.

"There was a small staff of people here and I went through a succession of positions and enjoyed learning with the company," she said. "There was a long lead time during pipeline construction and I talked with engineers and draftsmen as the work progressed. Visitors continually came to the office asking questions about the pipeline.

"Finally the company moved me to the Captain Cook Hotel where I became an information center for the pipeline—on my own, making presentations to organizations such as service clubs and writing scripts for slide programs for the schools. But when the pipeline was completed, they closed the office and reduced the staff. There appeared to be no prospects for advancement.

"So I went into business for myself. Since I'd made many contacts in my work with the pipeline, it wasn't difficult to secure clients. Courses in advertising and marketing research here in Anchorage were helpful. Now I need to improve my writing skills.

"I've formed a network with women in Alaska, and hire writers, photographers and graphic artists to help me complete work for my clients. For a time I took VIP visitors to Prudhoe Bay (the northern terminus of the pipeline)—flying up with them, taking them on a tour and flying back with them. Recently I prepared a 48-page brochure for the oil company. I liked doing that."

Now here was something to which I could relate. As I listened to Cheryl, I thought I'd like working here on public relations. I could see, however, that competition for the work would be keen. But I'd be willing to accept the challenge, I thought. Writing brochures about Prudhoe Bay would be much more fun than working on an oil rig. Not that hard physical labor was an option for me, but I knew that Dave was thinking about that option for himself as we had listened to Jim.

In exchange for the lifestyle here, both Cheryl and Jim are willing to put up with some inconveniences. Anchorage has many shortages that we hadn't thought about. "Like toilet paper, for instance," Cheryl said. "And you have to shop early for school supplies and clothing or else you're out of luck. We've sometimes had to resort to thrift stores and Salvation Army outlets for supplies. You have to make adjustments."

I don't often shop for fun; when I do go shopping, I like to be able to buy what I need on that particular day. Well, I could adjust to shortages, I suppose. I remember when butter, meat, shoes and gasoline were rationed during World War II, but I don't remember suffering as a result of the shortages. It might be different being an adult with teenagers. I wondered.

But Cheryl indicated that there were compensations for the inconveniences. "In Alaska in winter we watch the sun and note that we're gaining six minutes of sun a day," she countered.

Another thing I hadn't really faced—the fact that some days in the middle of winter there are really only a few hours of daylight. When autumn comes, I begin to resent the early darkness.

"I'm protecting what I've found here—a lifestyle," Jim

said. "There are strong personalities here. I suppose if too many people move North, Cheryl and I might push on to another frontier. I guess we'd like to sail around the world or work on inventions. But the air is clean here and I love playing golf in these surroundings. There's lots of beauty in Alaska. You could spend your life in this country and not see it all."

Yes, the beauty. The mountain vistas were getting a grip on me. They just might compensate for other inconveniences.

Boom town growing

We first met Rich Sewell in Kalamazoo when he was home visiting his family. Now we found him in his City Hall office in Anchorage. When Rich's regional planning job in southwest Michigan evaporated, he headed north to the largest city in Alaska, a city similar in size to Kalamazoo but with very different planning problems. Here, in the jet age, he found a modern-day paradox of the old western frontier with MacDonald's hamburgers.

"Half of all the people in Alaska live around Anchorage," he told us, "and the city has growing pains a-plenty."

Twenty-six year old Rich, who has a degree in economics, had been working for the Southcentral Michigan Regional Planning Commission until funding for his job ran out.

He was thinking of traveling to Europe after his layoff, but then heard about an opportunity in Alaska. Anchorage was looking for a regional economist for its Department of Planning, a description that fit Rich's training exactly. He applied for and got the job.

Rich says he has been in love with the rugged beauty of the North since he was a boy flying into the Canadian bush country to fish with his father and brother. So he was pleased with the opportunity to work in Anchorage.

"Job-hunters in Alaska need to be at the right place at the right time," Rich said. "Those who arrive without jobs need a

The spectacular view from Rich Sewell's office window.

big grub stake to carry them over." Professional and technical workers tend to be imported to the 49th state, we were told. Support jobs are filled locally.

We also learned that if you can stay with friends in Alaska, while you look for work, it helps because fifty dollar a day motel bills could eat up the savings of a job-seeker in no time.

Part of Rich's job at City Hall is to do research and provide data to politicians who ask: "Who are my constitutents and what services do they need and want?"

"Alaska is having frontier problems, and Anchorage is the classic boom town of the moment," Rich told us as we sat in his office in Anchorage overlooking skyscrapers and mountains. "Anchorage is having growing pains much like western towns of the past—Kansas City or St. Louis, for example.

"People in Anchorage are debating now where to put the opera house and where to locate the town square. Then there's the continuing debate between the advocates of growth and the Greenies.

"Greenies," he explained, "are environmentalists who say, 'Stay home; we don't want any more growth.'"

Also sensitive to environmental issues, Rich mentioned the Cassiar Highway, a scenic alternative to the Alcan Highway that goes through British Columbia, as being hit by "too much traffic and development."

Anchorage itself is a city that seems constantly under construction, with new office buildings and hotels being built downtown and posh new residential neighborhoods climbing up the mountainsides to the boundaries of the adjoining Chugach State Park.

With just under 250,000 people, Anchorage is a place where roof top restaurants overlook harbors and salmon-spawning streams, where migratory waterfowl nest in city park lakes and where residents joke about bear and moose wandering through their streets and yards.

One view from Rich's office includes snow covered mountains. In the other direction is Cook Inlet, which serves as an avenue into the city for Pacific Ocean boat traffic. On a clear day, you can see Denali (still referred to by traditionalists as Mt. McKinley), North America's highest mountain, 135 miles to the north.

But in closer focus are some social problems. "Unfortunately," Rich said, "many natives have become alcoholics because of oil royalties. They no longer need to hunt for food and skins for clothing and materials to trade, so they've resorted to drink because they've nothing else to do." But we learned, however, that concerned agencies have been making progress against this problem.

The winters affect not just residents of remote villages. Rich sees a need for a better balance in the recreational offerings in Anchorage where people tend to live at breakneck pace all summer when the days are extra long, and then hibernate through the dark winters. Critical needs, according to Rich, include more space for indoor court games such as volleyball and racquetball.

In the summer, however, Alaska has no shortage of recreational attractions. Rich's newest interest, when we talked with him last, was mountain climbing, and he was taking a college class to hone his skills in that sport.

Rich's qualifications could have landed him a good job anywhere. I sensed that he wouldn't hesitate to pursue a new challenge Outside eventually; but meanwhile Alaska provides him opportunities to add to his professional resume and to toughen his body.

A lifestyle to enjoy

As we prepared to leave Rich's office, he introduced us to Lisa Ameen. Sitting at the drawing board in City Hall with her reddish brown pigtails flung behind her, and wearing a green jersey blouse and blue jeans, the attractive, freckle-faced young woman was updating a map of the municipality.

Lisa is a graphic artist for the city of Anchorage. Her husband Robert, who had been a cost accountant in Flint, Michigan, has a degree in economics and hopes eventually to find a better job in Anchorage.

"My husband and I spent our first summer here fishing and camping—even though it was raining," she explained. "We drove up the Alcan in June with all of our belongings in our Ford camper truck, pulling our jeep."

"In Flint I didn't like the cars-cars-cars," Lisa said. "It sometimes took us three hours to drive from Flint to Saginaw on a weekend—and the two cities are less than 50 miles apart." Lisa had grown up in Montana and had lived in Marquette in Michigan's upper peninsula so she knew what wide open spaces were like.

Unlike some couples who preferred rural life, Lisa and Robert had elected to settle in the largest city in Alaska.

"We came to Anchorage first," she said, "because we thought there would more likely be jobs here. I found a job almost immediately—here at City Hall. It took Robert longer, but he's working for the municipality now—not doing exactly what he wants to do, but he'll find something in his field eventually."

Lisa and Robert like to hunt and fish, but Lisa says, "It's not realistic to stay in the bush and think you can live off the land. Wilderness living is a luxury. Some folks who go to the bush save up money to buy enough food for a year before they go. It takes money to live in the bush."

Living in Anchorage is expensive too. "We've been paying $410 for a one-bedroom apartment and the rent has just jumped to $525," Lisa reported. "We're thinking of buying a home in Palmer—forty miles away—and commuting to Anchorage. We can buy a house in Palmer for about $20,000 less than in Anchorage. Anchorage has nowhere to expand unless they build a bridge over Knik Arm." Lisa pointed out the window of her City Hall office, toward the waterway separating Anchorage from potential suburbs.

"We moved here to find a lifestyle as well as a job," Lisa added. "I'm glad we came."

I began to see that moving to Alaska would take more than courage. It would take money—lots of it. It would be hard to give up the home in the woods that Dave and I had built and moved into the year before. We'd need all of our equity to purchase a home in Alaska, and although we received many compliments from friends about our lovely home, I doubt any of them want to buy it. At least not for what we have invested.

As I thought about our new home, I decided that perhaps Dave and I already have the best of two worlds. We're secluded in the country—yet we can get to a concert, museum, art gallery, library, half a dozen theatres, three colleges and a university within thirty minutes.

Never look back

Isolation is okay for some individuals for a time; others could never conceive of living apart from the society they know. I don't think any of our children want to live away from "where the action is."

Dianne and Elliott Barske, however, feel they've discovered their ideal degree of solitude in the largest city in Alaska. Dianne is a 37-year old artist who moved to Anchorage from Boston with her husband ten years earlier. We listened to their story over lunch one rainy day.

"When we first stepped off the plane at Anchorage International Airport, I felt like a dog shaking the dust out of his coat," Dianne said. "This was to be a new life for us. I felt we were growing old back East," she said. "We're freer here. We don't have to deal with as many 'dos' and 'don'ts.'"

Eliott is a metereologist for the U. S. Weather Bureau. His job brought him and his family to Anchorage when he actively sought his own kind of work in the North country.

Dianne earned her master's in English education and has worked in public relations, but she really wants to paint.

"I've done a lot of landscapes. Now I want to do more people," she said. "I came to Alaska to write and to paint—and for adventure." Dianne was currently doing free lance writing and some painting in acrylics as well as serving as an administrative assistant in a public relations firm.

Unlike many Alaskans, these two have chosen not to separate themselves from society. Dianne is a member of the Alaska Press Women's organization and meets regularly with other writers. She was with three other Press Women who had joined us for lunch at this same restaurant the summer before.

Dianne and Elliott have found satisfaction living in the Alaskan city which has a pace much slower than the Lower 48. They appreciate the advantages of a large city; yet enjoy an independence they never experienced back home. They've taken up dog sled racing as a hobby and they love it.

"In Anchorage, if you have plastic money or enough cash, you can buy a leather jacket, a musk-ox yarn vest or a microwave oven," Dianne explained. "You can see a Hollywood movie or an audio-visual presentation about the history of Alaska. Within a few hours, you can fly nearly anywhere in the world. Travel agents are busiest in the winter—booking passage to Hawaii."

Five years later we spent another day with the couple. Elliott is still a meterologist. Dianne has had four one-person shows of her paintings in two years. She has also provided public relations services for an art gallery.

"I think I may investigate the possibility of making prints soon," Dianne said.

Their daughter Lee Ann, now 16, enjoys dog mushing competition while fourteen-year-old son Eric plays soccer and hockey. Ethan, the one-year-old, makes them all very happy as they enjoy watching him discover the world.

"We all knew when we left Boston that we'd never go back to stay," Dianne said. "We do go Outside every two years to visit our parents and spend some time in Connecticut in a trailer on the beach. While we're there, we go to museums and concerts, ride the subways—do everything we can't do in Anchorage.

"Then when we come back and go camping here in Alaska, I remember why our home is here," Dianne added.

The Barskes drove us south of Anchorage to the Portage Glacier where we visited the new Begich-Boggs Visitor Center. The center had just opened, and we, like everyone else, were very impressed. Huge displays explaining the history and geology of the area cover the walls of the center, an exceptionally good film about the changing glacier is shown several times each day and forest naturalists were available to answer questions.

A large paved parking area provides a view of the glacier and the floating blue-white icebergs in Portage Lake. It was raining the day we were there so we didn't take the self-guided moraine trail that begins just south of the center, but we made a note to return.

The drive is sometimes scary as the road runs along beside a drop off. There are mountains on one side and water below on the other. The tidal flats are interesting here, but dangerous. Individuals are cautioned not to venture out onto the mud flats at low tide for the incoming tide creates a quicksand effect, but the spectacular view is worth the trip. This is a delightful ride on week days, but on weekends, the traffic is often bumper to bumper. There's only a two-lane road between Anchorage and Seward, one of the few cities with a ferry terminal.

Look for it in the library

Dave and I had stopped at the library early one morning because we like libraries and because they're a good place to sit and catch up on what's going on in the world. There we met Beverlee Weston who was ready and eager to talk.

Beverlee found Anchorage to be a place where she could use her skills and also make a transition in her life. As head librarian at Mountain View, one of Anchorage's newest and most inviting branch libraries, she had worked through what she called a major "switch time".

The tall, athletic -looking woman appeared stern yet warm.

"I had experienced a second divorce and I wasn't satisfied with my job in the school where I was teaching," Beverlee began. "I wanted to move from the first grade classroom to the third grade and I wasn't given the opportunity."

The mother of two grown children, Beverlee had once worked for an industrial magazine, later became a teacher and then took leave to go to library school and then went back into the school system. (This was all in the Lower 48.)

"But my school library became a study hall dumping ground, she said, frowning as she spoke. "Kids were in the library thinking it was a prison. 'These kids will hate librarians and libraries forever,' I thought."

I could relate to that. Having had sometimes to supervise study halls, I knew that job could turn anyone off teaching forever. Study time belongs in the classroom with the teachers who assign the material—or at home.

Beverlee continued, "Finally I bought a Greyhound bus pass for $99 and visited every relative I knew."

As she spoke I could see a woman wearily lugging a suitcase on and off a bus. Yet, at the same time I could imagine the excitement she must have felt as she sped across the miles searching—I guess that's what Dave and I were doing now—searching. I could understand how she must have felt.

"I traveled two months and decided I wanted to work in a public library where I could help people who really care," she added.

After considerable correspondence, she found the right position in Anchorage.

"I want to work with people, to educate them, to provide alternatives for them, help them find information," Beverlee said. "My job here has been my total satisfaction. It gives me something that I care about."

Beverlee needed something to care about. Her second marriage lasted only a year and that had hurt.

"I like Alaska but I probably won't retire here," she offered. "I can't hike very far, and in winter it's very slippery. I've had back surgery. I'll probably move Outside by retirement time."

Five years later over breakfast in the Golden Lion restaurant in Anchorage we received an update on Beverlee's life. She was pleased that we had remembered her and had taken the time to look her up.

She and a friend, Nancy, had puchased a house in Eugene, Oregon and were in the process of moving.

Beverlee was looking forward to Oregon—with a new

concert center and living an hour from the ocean and an hour from summer theater and near her children and grandchildren.

"After thirteen years, I realize how isolated Alaska is when you're not involved with children in schools and sports," Beverlee said. "It's the darkness that gets me—not the cold. You have to be a total outdoor winter sport freak to make it here. Full spectrum lights in my office helped.

Beverlee Weston

"Nancy and I don't cross-country ski. The young people do. Everything is geared to the young."

One outlet for Beverlee has been the Richard III Society. "We feel that King Richard has been badly maligned," she said. "He ruled England from 1367-1400 and in Shakespeare's play he is made out to be a real villain. Our group studies his life and reign in an attempt to improve his negative image."

Beverlee has also traveled throughout the state, attending library conferences at both local and state levels. And she has watched many people come and go in The Great Land.

"People with skills stay," she offered. "Those with no skills, union membership, or local contacts may have trouble. If you want to live in Alaska, it's important to come and apply for a driver's license, voter's registration, library card, credit card and establish residence immediately. Apply for the dividends available to permanent residents. Get involved and develop credibility as an Alaskan.

"It's becoming easier to find housing, but be aware of expenses. If you like to fish, realize that fishing is only a few months a year. People who like artists' colonies may want to check out Homer as a possible place to settle."

"I've camped, hiked, fished and flown," she said. "I flew to Mount McKinley and landed on the glacier. I took river raft trips and flying lessons. I've shown lots of visitors around the state. It has been an incredible thirteen years. Now it's time to leave."

I envied Beverlee her years in Alaska. It sounded as though she had tried it all. I love cross-country skiing. So, I wondered, what's keeping me in lower Michigan where there's seldom enough snow?

The Kenai

"Coming to Alaska was the best thing I ever did," said Judy Mullen who grew up in Duluth, Minnesota. "I wouldn't change it although I didn't plan to end up here. Places without mountains don't seem right to me any more."

The 30-year old blonde, hair pulled back into a pony tail, sat typing catalog cards behind the circulation desk at the Mountain View branch of the Anchorage Public Library.

Judy's comment about mountains caught my attention, for Dave and I had been grappling with the feeling—wondering what there was about mountains. They did seem to have a magnetic quality about them.

"In 1970, I was 18 and very independent," Judy continued. "I had been awarded a scholarship to attend the University of Minnesota in St. Paul, but I didn't like the big city community. It seemed cold and impersonal, and I was just another person running back and forth. So I turned down the scholarship and got myself a cabin near Duluth on the shore of Lake Superior and lived alone with my dog and commuted to a philosophy class at a nearby small college.

"One day my friend Mary came to visit and said, 'You'd better come to Alaska with me.'

"I said, 'no' but she brought pictures she'd cut from *Alaska* magazine and put them on the wall. Later Mary returned, this time driving an old Plymouth that she had bought for $40.

"She announced, 'I'm going to Alaska. You're coming with me.'

"I said, 'You can't go in that old car.'

"'Then we'll take yours,' Mary responded, and began tossing her belongings from her car into mine.

"My philosophy course final exam was the next day. I took the test, dropped my stereo off at my mother's home in Duluth and went with Mary.

"We started out with two guitars, two puppies, a cot, our knapsacks and two woolen blankets that Mary insisted we purchase from the Salvation Army. I thought the blankets were silly, but they came in handy later.

"Before we reached Canada, we had picked up another woman—a friend of Mary's, who after much deliberation, had decided to leave her husband and children." The woman later returned to her family, but meanwhile she traveled with Judy and Mary.

Judy said, "I love my family, but we don't have strong family ties. I write to them and send them pictures; but I don't need to be with them all of the time.

"I surprised my friends and my brother though. They weren't expecting me to take off for the unknown."

I thought of my own "journey into the unknown." Big deal. I'd gone off by myself to teach in California right after graduation from college. But relatives lived in the city where I went to teach. My father's cousin met me at the train and invited me to stay with her and her family until I found a place. I ended up rooming for the school year with my mother's cousin and his wife and daughter.

Going across the country was a big step for me when I was 21, but having relatives there to greet me helped. Going to

Alaska would have seemed impossible. Now I felt myself wishing I had been even braver back then and applied for a teaching job in Alaska after the year in California. I envied Judy her pluck.

Judy continued, "I didn't know what I was doing. I had $60. The three of us spent five weeks getting to Alaska, stopping at all of the cafes and gas stations along the Alcan Highway. We never got hurt or in trouble and I continued to mail cards and letters home.

"Finally my VW blew up because I didn't know enough to add oil to the engine. By then, we were near Hope, on the Kenai Peninsula, and so I sold the car for $100; and the three of us—Mary, our other friend and I started hitchhiking.

"A truck driver who gave us a ride said he needed somebody to help him pick up rocks. We learned later that he always picked up hitchhikers to help him collect shale to use as skirting for trailers. There was lots of shale on this road to Hope so we really earned our ride.

"As I was picking up shale, I thought—what am I doing—slinging this rock? But now I know why. Because the truck driver was Ted, a fellow about ten years my senior, who later became my husband."

Ted was born in the Phillipines, grew up in San Francisco and was introduced to Alaska by the United States Army. The Army shipped Ted back to the lower 48, but as soon as he earned his discharge papers in 1951, he bought a car intending to drive back up the Alcan. But after totaling his car, Ted ended up in Alaska with only 23 cents in his pocket. Thirty-one years later he was still here.

"After the rock slinging, Ted introduced us to an Alaskan native family who owned a cabin where we could stay," Judy recalled. "I got a morning job cleaning the bar in an inn outside Soldotna. The woman bar owner took a liking to me and invited me to move into her extra cabin closer to my work.

"Meanwhile, for fun, I was going fishing with Ted," Judy said. "He taught me how to catch salmon in a gill net and how to handle a boat. But it wasn't always fun. One of my most horrible memories is of being in the boat—in heavy seas—making tomato sandwiches for Ted and another fisherman. The thought of food was revolting. I spent most of my time with my head hanging over the edge of the boat."

"Ted also ran a trapline and so we thought we'd make some extra money selling furs," Judy said. "We spent a winter in another friend's cabin outside of Soldotna. But not enough animals came to our traps. We were lucky to have Ted's salmon money to see us through the winter.

"A lot of folks on the Kenai Peninsula live seasonal lives. They fish all summer or work on construction or oil drilling, shoot a moose in the fall and then 'lay dead' all winter.

"Because of some difficulty with paperwork, Ted hadn't received his limited entry fishing permit and so that took away any hope of his operating a commercial fishing boat," Judy explained. "Cost of fishing permits is now out of reach.

"So Ted went into construction work," Judy said. "We rented an old shack that we fixed up to look like a log cabin. We put in insulation and with Ted's chain saw, we cut a hole in the wall large enough to fit an enormous bargain sale picture window.

"That window was a good investment—it brightened our whole outlook on Alaska. Some mornings we could sit there in front of the window and observe as many as 80 moose browsing the willows. One day a lynx strolled by our window. Another morning, we watched a wolf steal a frozen salmon right off our porch."

How neat to be able to watch wildlife so closely, I thought. But repair an old cabin? Now that's something I'd like to be able to say I had done, but I'm not sure I'd choose to do it.

"That was a good berry year," Judy continued, "so we picked and preserved a lot of them. That was also my 'back to college' year. I took courses in geology and writing at Kenai Peninsula Community College."

"Ok," I thought. "I could go for this back-to-college stuff

anytime."

Judy continued. "For three seasons Ted and I set out gill nets and we also did contract commercial fishing for an old fellow who owned a permit for a site outside Soldotna.

"Those were good years. For the first time we actually watched Cook Inlet freeze, noting how the ice inched its way out from the shore and came back onto the beach in chunks and slabs. The pieces of ice grew with each incoming tide until some became giant ice boulders.

"The oil stove in our shack often clogged up, but we had electricity and we put in an indoor cesspool.

"During that period I learned how much snow you have to melt to wash your hair," recalled Judy. "We had a sink but no running water.

"And as I remember, the good times weren't connected with money," Judy said. "Oh, of course, you have to have some money."

As she spoke about money, I thought how often what we do is determined by money or by the security that money brings. Given no monetary restrictions, what would most of us really do with our time? The cost of our trip to Alaska had been a dilemma. We had spent hours debating if we should really spend the money. Weren't there other things we wanted and needed? Perhaps, but nothing was needed so much at this time in our lives, as it had been for Judy Mullen, as a trip to Alaska.

From Soldotna, Judy and Ted moved to Seward where Judy cut up salmon in a cannery—when work was available.

"I lived in Seward two years," Judy said, "but I never felt really welcome. Seems to me that the community had made a choice not to accept outsiders.

"I also worked in a restaurant in Seward. It was hard work, but interesting. All of the regulars, local folks, came in. And although I was hired as a waitress, sometimes the cook/dishwasher would get drunk and I'd have to fill in for him.

"Drinking is a real problem in many parts of Alaska. Most

of the people I'd see were drinking or smoking dope. I didn't want to do that so I had very few friends.

"That was a difficult time. Something was missing, and part of the time it was Ted who was missing." Judy and Ted weren't yet married, but somehow they began to feel that they belonged together. Ted had yielded to the temptation of Black Gold.

The Aleyeska pipeline project paid such good wages that men from all over Alaska and the Lower 48 left whatever they were doing to join the construction crews during those four hectic years of 1972-1976. Sometimes Ted was among them.

But Judy recalled a more pleasant time working with Ted, harvesting kelp in Prince William Sound.

"Fish eggs or roe aren't a popular food in the U. S., but the Japanese eat them like candy. Caviar is actually a kind of roe, but the taste never really caught on except in the Orient and in Europe. We would cut the roe from where it had been deposited on the kelp and pack it into small boxes. We got ourselves soaking wet wading out after the seaweed, but fifty cents a pound seemed like good pay at the time and we thought we were getting rich."

Then Judy told us about the summer she and Ted spent squeezing herring. "The trick was to identify the female fish, grab hold of her in just the right place and squeeze out the roe," Judy explained.

"Herring eggs are an expensive delicacy. Orientals love them. The problem with herring is that the roe won't come out when the fish is fresh so you have to let them age a few days. Then you have to squeeze the roe out of rather well seasoned herring." The carcass of the fish ends up as pet food.

"The stench in the packing plant was so terrible that we could hardly breathe; but since it was piece work, if we worked fast, we could make $100 a day.

"I was the first squeezer in the family, but Ted joined me when he saw how much money he could make. He soon became the fastest squeezer in the place. We developed a knack for picking out the females and came up with a certain rhythm—pick, squeeze, toss.

"We squeezed herring 12 hours a day and it was fun. We'd sing, talk and tell tall tales. We even got used to the smell. Now this work is all mechanized with conveyer belts; but in those days, fellows actually carried baskets of fish around."

Hard work didn't bother Judy; but the long dark winters did.

"It was eight winters after I left Minnesota before I went back Outside. Then it was to visit San Francisco," she said. "Finally Ted and I moved to Anchorage and I began working at the Learning Resources Center at Anchorage Community College. I was an aide in the learning lab, did some tutoring and helped foreign students with writing. I enjoyed that. I also clerked in a drugstore.

"Then I decided to take a trip to Europe; but I realized I'd have to earn more money to be able to go, so I looked for another job. I ended up here at this library; and after working a year, I got two months off so Ted and I could go to Europe. Before we went, we got married."

After their European trip, the couple returned to Anchorage and have remained there.

Judy said that Ted continues to do construction work in the summers, but "lays dead" in the winter. Besides working on the pipeline, he helped build the Seward Highway and the fish hatchery on the northern edge of Trail Lake.

"I want variety in my life," Judy said. "Although I was never comfortable in a giant metropolis, I like having some of the city pleasures—like the symphony and the theater. I like my job here in the library; but I get a craving to be in the woods. I like the wilderness. I want electric lights and running water, yet I'd rather live in a cabin in the woods than in a town house.

"We have a lot of material things here. Especially after having been to Europe, I realize what a soft life I have. What's more, I like the space in Alaska. Even though Anchorage is a city, I can get to the country very quickly.

"I miss my family back in Minnesota and I hope my dad and stepsister will come to visit us this fall. I'm afraid Alaska still doesn't exist as a real place for my mother. I don't know if she'll ever come to visit me here."

"We like to go Outside, but we're glad to get back to Alaska," Judy said. "There's a fresh feeling here. It's cold, but it's clear, fresh and invigorating. And there's a mystique here."

I knew how Judy felt. She savors the out-of-doors, but she also enjoys a new car and a microwave oven. I felt I'd made a friend as I listened to Judy Mullen. Somehow I felt we'd meet again and would sometime find ourselves sitting across a table drinking tea with her and Ted.

"You'll be back," Judy said. And I believed her. If the spell of the land wasn't strong enough to lure us, people like Judy would be. Then as a final gesture to cement our friendship, she took from the shelves a paperback novel about the building of the Alaska pipline, handed it to us, saying, "Here, take this with you. We have several copies and it will give you some insight about the pipeline era."

For Judy, mountains make the difference. "There were no mountains in Minnesota," mused Judy. "There was water and wildlife, but no mountains. I never dreamed I would spend most of my life on the edge of the Arctic; but here I am, and places without mountains just don't seem right to me anymore."

The Arctic

"I've done ten times as much with my life here in Nome as I probably would have done in Michigan," Leo Rasmussen told us from behind the cash register at the Music Mart. Since coming to Alaska in 1962, Leo has served on the city council and had just been elected to a third term as mayor of the isolated northwest coastal city of Nome, less than 200 miles across the Bering Strait from Siberia.

After spending several days in Anchorage, Dave and I had been eager to see other parts of the state—some of which would be accessible only by air.

The idea of going to Nome had always intrigued me—probably because we couldn't get there by automobile. When my friend Sue Moore, of Vicksburg, a community of 2,200 in southwestern Michigan, told me about Leo Rasmussen, a hometown boy who grew up to be mayor of Nome, I was determined to find him so I called him from Anchorage. We then booked ourselves on a tour crossing the Arctic Circle to Nome and Kotzebue with overnight accomodations at the Nome Nugget Inn.

Leo's wife Erna, a native of Norway, served us a delicious

dinner in their home which included broiled salmon and for dessert—an authentic baked Alaska. We felt royally treated, and our host and hostess were generous with information as well as with food.

Leo and Erna had an eight-month-old adopted daughter at the time we visited them, and we've since learned that they've adopted another daughter. They had also just finished extensively expanding and remodeling their home.

"For weeks we worked all night in the midnight sun," Erna said. The time appeared to have been well spent, for their home is lovely. A beamed, high-ceilinged living room with a balcony overlooking it provides a showplace for their collection of paintings and wall hangings. China plates, ivory carvings and many other artifacts—some peculiar to the North and others which have been given them by parents and friends—add to the tasteful decor.

Remodeling their home was just one of many challenges for Leo. He thrives on activity, and there appears to be as much potential for activity in Nome as anywhere else.

Leo and Erna own and manage "The Music Mart," a thriving business in a town where months of winter darkness and isolation create a demand for records, cassettes, stereo equipment and musical instruments.

Leo has also been a gold miner, spent some time on the North Slope in oil exploration, campaigned for the office of state senator, served as vice chairman of the Republican Party in Alaska and still finds time for woodworking.

He is also active on the committee that sponsors the annual Iditarod sled dog racing marathon and is a writer and founding director of the *Bering Straights*, a weekly newspaper published in Nome.

Although the pioneering era passed in Vicksburg, Michigan decades before Leo was born, Leo finds that the frontier lifestyle continues in Nome.

"We're just coming out of the nineteenth century," Leo said of the town founded as a gold miners' camp in 1898.

Leo Rasmussen says, "I've done far more here in Nome than I could ever have done Outside."

Nearly 30,000 miners, saloon-keepers, gamblers and soldiers of fortune arrived in 1899 and 1900 creating a city five miles long and two blocks wide. Some say there were 100 saloons in that city.

"Even today not all of the town has water and sewer service," Leo said. He pointed out, however, that since outdoor privies are both illegal and impractical, lavatories are indoors with holding tanks which have to be empied regularly by "honey" trucks that remove the waste for sanitary disposal.

The mayor said there were 2,100 winter-time residents of Nome, but in summer that figure swells to 3,600 when fishing and mining activity pick up. Another 2,000 people—mostly Eskimos, live in isolated villages along the coast and on the tundra surrounding the city.

Front Street, Nome's dusty, graveled main road, is only a glance away from the Bering Sea. Great boulders, piled high at the edge of town, protect the shoreline from violent northwesterly storms that blow in off the seas such as the fierce blast of 1974 that engulfed many buildings along this street.

Many of the city's dwellings are tin-roofed shacks or wood framed houses. A number of buildings tilt at odd angles because of annual thawing and refreezing of the soil. Some of the construction is a foot or two above the soil line because a home built directly on the ground can thaw the permanently frozen subsoil causing the dwelling to sink.

A sideline the Rasmussens operate—they're agents for the Alaska Pacific Grocery—points up another curiosity of Alaskan life and another of the challenges facing the city. Area residents come to the Music Mart to pick up a catalog from which they can order groceries through Rasmussens' mail order operation.

Leo says catalog users can save one third to one half by purchasing by the case, but even then, a typical year's grocery bill for a family of five can run up to about $5,000. The tab includes fresh milk at $1.99 a half gallon, and oranges and bananas at forty to fifty cents apiece.

High prices reflect high freight costs, so Leo was promoting a new $35 million port facility for the city which would eliminate having to transfer all cargo from ships to barges as is done now.

Nome is accessible only by air, snow machine or dog sled in the winter. In summer the city can be reached by sea, but there is no highway to the Outside. Although a few residents have shipped in autos for local transportation, most citizens here would like to see a railroad line constructed—not a highway.

"A railroad would have greater capabilities and maintenance costs would be less," Leo told us.

Transportation charges affect fuel oil prices as they do food prices, so people in Nome often burn driftwood to conserve oil.

There's no standing timber in this tundra country, for once roots get through the few inches of topsoil, they're unable to penetrate the rock-hard permafrost. Much of the winter fuel for Nome homes floats hundreds of miles down the Yukon River from Alaska's interior and from the forests of western Canada. Spruce and cedar logs end up sprawled on the rocky beaches outside of town, becoming fuel for the picking by cost conscious Nome homeowners.

"But the fact that there are only two or three living vertical trees in the whole city was one of the things that impressed me on my first visit to this spot," Leo said with a grin. "I knew nobody could sneak up on me."

Leo recalls that when he was a student at the University of Alaska in Fairbanks, he was assigned to Nome for the summer as a protection aide with the Department of Fish and Game. "You could see across the horizon," he said. "I decided then that this place couldn't be all bad."

After subsisting on peanut butter sandwiches through the next two semesters, Leo gave up school for awhile and packed his bags again for Nome. He hasn't been sorry.

The appeal of the place is as simple as the delight on an

arctic summer night when the sky is bright well past midnight, and as satisfying as the freedom of knowing that there are few barriers for anyone who wants to make a mark.

"There's so much to be done," Leo said.

Nome seems to be Alaska in miniature. Although the state is twice as large as Texas, there are fewer people living in Alaska than in the city of El Paso. Leo says that in Alaska it isn't easy to disappear into the woodwork—or into the woods. People are known from village to village.

"In Alaska, people work together, even if they don't like one another," Leo said. "You know that eventually you'll have to cooperate with almost everybody else around."

Having traveled around Alaska extensively, mostly for political meetings, Leo has concluded that he would like to run for the office of governor if campaign money were available. His interest in politics was nourished on frequent convention trips with his father, a physician, who for many years was coroner of Kalamazoo County in Michigan.

Leo said, "My first political experience was at a cherry festival where Michigan's Governor G. Mennen Williams patted me on the head after I'd been an Indian on a float in the festival parade. It made me feel good when the governor said, 'Hello, Dr. Rasmussen, and how is little Leo?' I was impressed."

Talk of Alaska and his visions of its future come easily to Rasmussen, but there's more to his life. "When you're faced with life-threatening situations, you come to know yourself," Leo said.

Because Nome is the closest U. S. city to the Soviet Union, several times Leo has become involved in international incidents. In 1983, for example, seven members of the environmental group Greenpeace were arrested by the Soviets after sailing into Siberian waters in an attempt to prove that whale meat was being used to feed fur animals in the Soviet Union.

Leo, then mayor of Nome, served as the official U. S. representative who met with the Soviets to sign papers for the release of those arrested and then returned with the seven to Nome aboard the Greenpeace ship, *Rainbow Warrior*.

I found myself envying Leo and Erna their remote environment even though I'd earlier thought that Anchorage was the only place in Alaska I'd want to live. Leo and Erna were "big fish" in a little pond. Leo was known all over Alaska. I didn't think it was fame I was seeking, and I wasn't interested in becoming a politician, but don't we all have a feeling that we'd like to make a difference somewhere for something or someone?

Maybe, I felt, it would be possible to make a significant difference in Nome. I could be a newspaper reporter. Or maybe I could be the local correspondent for some of the world's major newspapers. Why not aim high? How much competition can there be in Nome for stringers for the *New York Times*? Actually I might have been surprised at the number of opportunities had I taken the time to look further. But to live on a barren shoreline with no trees? I wasn't sure how I'd get along without trees.

We returned to Anchorage and continued to use that city for a time as the takeoff point for our next excursions.

We've since learned that Leo resigned his position as mayor to run for state Senate in 1986. Rugged individualism, a belief in hard work, private enterprise and non-interference by the government bureaucracy are important to him. Although Leo didn't win the election, he received 37% of the vote which he felt was good considering that he ran against a long time incumbent. And then there's always another time.

The Haul Road

Bob, a neatly dressed man of about forty, sports the most dapper mustache and owns one of the best looking rigs on the Dalton Highway. Behind the wheel of his blue and chrome

Peterbilt, which to truckers is like a Cadillac is to automobile drivers, Bob was making regular runs on the grueling strip of gravel that parallels the pipeline north of Fairbanks, across the Arctic Circle, to supply the oil drilling crews at Prudhoe Bay on the shore of the Arctic Ocean.

Yes, Dave and I were on the road again. We had set out from Fairbanks to drive the Dalton Highway, otherwise known simply as the North Slope Haul Road. "Just for the experience," Dave insisted.

I had not felt a need to experience the dusty Haul Road, but I liked the idea of being able to say I had done it, so I went along for the ride.

The road was rugged and we had been warned that there would be few gas stations so we pulled in at the first station we found. It was like a desert oasis surrounded by parked 18-wheelers. Half a dozen drivers were chatting with one another. Dave went and introduced himself to the truckers while I wandered into the little store.

Here one could fill the gas tank, replenish the coffee thermos and buy a bag of potato chips. Since we had our usual supply of dried fruit, granola bars and cans of V-8 juice, we didn't buy any food, but I looked carefully at the groceries. If we had really needed something, we could have purchased a can of peaches, a box of cake mix, a can of spaghetti or some tea bags.

Trucker talk

Dave learned that one of the truckers had come to Alaska in 1973 to haul for the pipeline. The trucker grossed $500,000 a year then—being paid $6,000 a load, and the company paid for the gas.

"Yes, I came from Montana for the money," he said. "Teamsters had no work in Montana as logging was closing down there. Now only half of the truckers in Alaska belong to the union, and we get only half as much pay per load and our operating costs have tripled. But I'm still making more money than I could in the Lower 48.

"There's room for a person to make a good living here," he said. "Three out of four truckers are owner-operators. Everybody knows everybody else. If you have a good reputation, you'll get work. It's important to be on time, to be clean and to always get through."

Professional truckers say the Haul Road, like the infamous Alcan, is better in winter when the surface is smoothly packed snow instead of loose gravel and potholes. However, drivers have to be prepared to wait out a blizzard anytime and then to continue on through the drifts to make their delivery. But there are fringe benefits. One driver said subsistence fishing and hunting provide him with opportunities to get extra meat for his family.

The code of the country outside the city limits is "Live and let live," said one trucker. "You can kill a moose if and when you need it for subsistence."

Likewise, it was money that brought Gary to Alaska. A short fellow with curly black hair, dark brown eyes and lots of enthusiasm, he specializes in hauling groceries from Anchorage to Prudhoe Bay.

Because he's away from his family a great deal, he takes his stepsons with him on his hauls during their summer vacation from school. The trucker's own children live with his ex-wife who spent one winter in Alaska and then left with the kids.

"I'm home with my family four days a week and on the road the other three," he explained. "I make good money—almost as much in one trip as most truckers make in two runs. Yes, there's opportunity in Alaska for a man to make his own way if he'll do it."

Money and independence

For some workers Alaska means money, nothing else. In the beginning, Glenn was escaping from a bad marriage. An electronics technician, he took a job in Alaska to get away from the memories, to earn enough cash to pay for his divorce and to get himself back on his feet.

Working for civilian contractors who maintain radar sites for the government, Glenn is flown wherever he wants to go, courtesy of the company. Unlike many of the people we met, Glenn has no desire to settle in Alaska. "I just want to make enough money so I can head for Florida where I can go deep sea fishing," he explained.

But money isn't the only reason people were on the Haul Road. At the Yukon River bridge we met Larry Dodge. It was late in the day, and the log sheet in the construction trailer that was serving as a temporary visitors' center showed that we were only the second vehicle to stop that day.

Independence is important to Larry, nearing forty, who lives in a tent along the Yukon River in the summer and spends winters hiking from camp to camp to check his 30 miles of trapline.

This summer the State offered him a job manning the visitors' center. "I live alone now," Larry said. "But I want to see people sometimes, so I took this job. I enjoy the summer, but by fall I'll be ready to go back to the bush and my trapline. But to make money trapping, I'd have to expand my line to at least 100 miles.

"I can get along without much money," Larry said, "but I'm not sure I can get along without people." At this point he says he has no one, but he enjoys a certain amount of freedom and independence that he didn't have before coming North.

"When you're alone, there's no one else to blame, and you have to start facing yourself and accepting responsibility for the things you do and the way you feel," he said. Larry is lonely. He also feels an urge to leave a mark, but he regrets that so far he has left, as he put it, "nothing but footprints in the snow."

On that rainy July day we left our footprints in mud at the Arctic Circle. Walking on the tundra gave me an eerie feeling—as if I were on the moon. Here I was in a place where few people had been. Was that what I wanted? If I wanted money, there would be easier ways to earn it than by uprooting my family and moving to Alaska. Was I then craving a uniqueness—wanting to be the only one who had done something? Was that important to me? To Dave?

These were questions I asked myself as I stretched my legs on the tundra for those few minutes before we got back into our pickup for the return drive to Fairbanks and on to Denali National Park.

The Interior

After returning to Fairbanks, we set out for Anchorage by way of the George Parks Highway and Denali National Park and Preserve. We spent the first night in a private campground a few miles from the park.

Campsites in the park are in great demand; but when we realized we had to get in line early in the day, we secured a good spot. We'd been told that we probably wouldn't see the top of 20,320 ft. Mount McKinley, North America's highest mountain. On a clear day the mountain is visible more than 200 miles away, but in rainy, cloudy summer weather, the chance of seeing the peak even once from inside the park is only about 40%.

Alaskans refer to the mountain as Denali which means *the big one* or *the great one*. Although the mountain didn't "come out" for us while we were in the park, we did enjoy a magnificent view of the summit from the air one purple and gold February morning.

Denali Park stands out among America's scenic splendors and wildlife wonders, but on this summer trip we were observing people in the park as well as the animals. We rode the yellow National Park Service bus deep into the wilderness on roads where private cars are prohibited.

We were reminded that in December 1980 with the passage of the Alaska Lands Bill, Mount McKinley National Park became part of Denali National Park and Preserve. The new park includes the original two million acres plus an additional 3.9 million acres protected from development.

The park teems with arctic wildlife including grizzly bears, caribou, red fox, moose, wolves, Dall sheep, marmots, pikas, ground squirrels and migratory birds. Lichens, mosses, low growing shrubs and colorful wild flowers cover the alpine tundra uplands.

Denali Park is the kind of place that, when you get there, you wish you had allotted two weeks instead of two days. It was not out of ignorance that we scheduled so little time, but because we wanted to see as much of Alaska as possible in the two months we had to spend. We also knew that nearly everyone who visits Alaska includes Denali Park on their itinerary, and we hoped to spend as much time as possible in less-traveled places and to talk with local people.

After the official Denali Park orientation presentation, we cornered Forest Ranger Robert Quinn who had come from New York state. This was his third summer in the park, and his wife Janet was also a ranger there.

Robert knows what he wants. He wants to help shape the future of Alaska. He has a forestry degree and legislative experience as research director in the New York State Senate. He knows and cares about natural resources and wildlife and wants to balance protection with accessibility and public enjoyment.

"We need some kind of balance in our lives," he said. "I enjoy people and the variety cities have to offer. I worked at a desk three years, and I liked it, but the work was very intense so I came up here to get away from more conventional things. Here we live in a one-room 14 x 14-foot cabin, 12 miles out in the park.

"If I can find a job, I'll stay in Alaska this fall," Robert said. "I might like to be in politics here; but if I can't find work, I'll return to New York." That seemed like a sensible decision.

It was in the gift shop at Denali that my usually frugal husband splurged on a soapstone bear. Dave had been carefully studying native carvings throughout our trip, but when he saw this lifelike, ten-inch long polar bear carved by a St. Lawrence Island native craftsman, he knew it was what he'd been looking for.

Eskimo artists carefully examine each piece of soapstone, jade or granite before beginning to carve—it's said they're seeking to release the spirit residing within the stone. Our olive green and black bear strides purposefully across the ice. His left front and right rear legs are raised in frozen motion. He appears to have a definite destination. There's no indecision here. I surmised that was what Dave liked about the carving in addition to its being a beautiful artistic creation.

As Dave made his purchase, I looked carefully at many of the other items in the park gift shop and decided that here were some of the best quality souvenirs we'd seen.

Denali Park would be a great place to spend an entire summer exploring the tundra and stalking wildlife; but it would mean leaving family and friends behind and abandoning clients. I wasn't sure I was ready to do that.

More important than money

Fred and Jeanne Ickes appeared to have adjusted to the "leaving it all behind" syndrome. Fred's blue jeans and plaid flannel shirt seemed to be the ideal uniform for living in the bush although they would have looked just as appropriate on a college campus. Jeanne, too, looked comfortable in her blue jeans and navy sweat shirt.

"You have to be flexible if you're going to stay in Alaska,"

Fred said, leaning forward in the straight-backed dining room chair. He and Jeanne were high school sweethearts at Kalamazoo Central where they both graduated in 1968. Going to Alaska seemed like a fun thing to do in 1976 so they packed up their belongings and three young children and took off for the North. Fred's parents already had roots down in Alaska so it wasn't as if the young family would be alone. Fred tended bar in his father's restaurant and motel in Talkeetna, known as the Gateway to Denali Park, about 100 miles north of Anchorage.

"Dad's partnership dissolved the next year so I tended bar in another place," Fred told us." Then I got a job as a laborer with The Corps of Engineers. When I was laid off there, I began working in a gas station and later was employed on an oil rig.

"The wages here are low compared to the pipeline," Fred said. "I get only $4 to $6 an hour. It isn't much, but we don't think money is worth my being away from Jeanne and the kids. You may get financial stability but lose your family. The crisis at home may come up the week you're on the Slope."

Fred said that any money left over from living expenses is invested in their home. They pay as they go, not wanting to owe anything on their house or land. Since it cost them $4,425 to have their well drilled, it was another year before they could afford to pipe water into the house.

"Everybody who comes here and builds their own place waits for water and plumbing," Jeanne said. "But the beauty is worth it, and we don't have social pressure here to have a fancy house."

The couple and their three pre-teen age children live in hilly forest land seven miles from Talkeetna. Some days in the winter they don't get into town because the road is closed.

"We used to plow our own road," Fred said. "Now the State maintains it, but we don't have it plowed unless it's really necessary because we know that when the government pays for something, that means we're all paying for it."

To Fred and Jeanne Ickes, family values are more important than money.

Fred had built three houses and was teaching himself to estimate in advance what a house will cost so he could become a contractor.

"If I had the money, I'd build homes on speculation," Fred said. "But I have a conflict. I want to build, but I don't want to build too much or the area will grow too much. I've thought of moving to southeastern Alaska, but then we'd need a boat and it would take several years to get re-established."

Jeanne was a teacher's aide in Talkeetna at the school their children attend.

"I'd like to get certified to teach and be able to do the planning myself," Jeanne said as she gazed through their picture window toward the mountains beyond. "But I'd need to go to Anchorage or back Outside to get the training."

"I could use some bookkeeping courses," Fred said. "I believe you can learn many things on the job, but some things can be learned faster in school. However, I don't have money to go to college now."

As he sat on the floor, Fred mused, "Our biggest expense

here is electricity. We buy groceries in Wasilla once or twice a month; occasionally we go to Anchorage for dinner or to a movie."

"I like being near a small town," Jeanne added. "I like knowing the people I see at the grocery store, yet I prefer not having neighbors really close.Our kids have each other. They can ride their bikes down the highway without fear of much traffic, and they're in a classroom with only 15 other kids instead of 30. Our TV hasn't worked for a long time, but I don't know when we'd have time to watch it. Now our kids are begging to go bowling and roller skating."

From the picture window in their A-frame home, on a clear day, Fred and Jeanne can see the outline of the Alaska mountain range framed with tall spruce trees. Mountains are one of the attractions that keep them in Alaska.

"We're not pioneers," Fred said. "We're not really living in the bush. But people are different here. When a neighbor's house burned down, we all got together and framed another house for them in a short time."

Fred added, "If you're thinking about getting rich quick, don't come to Alaska—unless you're a big business man. It takes a great deal of money to get started."

Fred and Jeanne don't have a lot of money but they're flexible. Perhaps flexibility is more important than money.

About the capital

After we heard about Willow, we wanted to visit there. The little unincorporated town of 200 people on the George Parks Highway between Anchorage and Denali Park was being proposed as a compromise site for a new state capital.

We learned that gold had been discovered in the area in 1897 and that mining slacked off in the 1940's leaving Willow a ghost town of sorts. But when the new highway was completed in 1972, Willow was back on the map.

Land speculation went rampant when Alaskans voted in 1976 to move the seat of the state government to Willow from foggy Juneau. But by 1982 the sharp decline in oil revenues had shelved the move and voters finally defeated funding.

"If you take the newspaper off the rack, you've bought it," warned the sign at Ellie's Cafe in Willow. A news stand plus a counter full of gifts and souvenirs supplemented cafe owner Ellie Wodkowski's income.

Although the modest rough-frame establishment contains only five tables, the menu appears to be "big city." We had a choice of an $8.95 halibut dinner, a $14.95 T-bone steak or a captain's platter of fish, shrimp, scallops and oysters also for $14.95. For the less hearty appetite there was a steak sandwich with potato salad, macaroni salad or soup of the day.

Even in this idyllic setting, the proprietor said she felt restless. "Ten years is long enough to be in the food business," Ellie said as she brought out bowls of steaming bean soup. She explained that she didn't want to leave the town; she was just tired of being tied down.

Ellie is also a musician who plays in a nearby roadhouse. Her husband is in the excavation business and there seemed to be plenty of new work in the area as well as recreational opportunities.

"Tourists fish for salmon and trout in the many lakes around here and there's lots to do in the winter," Ellie said. "We have a winter carnival with a queen and a pageant the last week in January and the first weekend of February. There are always snowmobiles and dog sleds to get around when the snow is deep."

Willow boasts seven churches: two Baptist and one each of Methodist, Catholic, Mormon, Seventh Day Adventist and an interdenominational chapel. Business establishments clustered along the edge of the Parks Highway include a public library, video rental shop, gas station, grocery which offers soft ice cream and a hardware store that sells "everything."

The main line of the Alaska Railroad runs straight through

the east side of town and the old depot still stands. Displayed on a bulletin board outside the post office were notices about a rummage sale, a two-bedroom, one bath house with a mountain view for rent for $595 a month and Alcoholics Anonymous meetings in the Willow Library.

After having a bowl of soup in Ellie's restaurant and chatting with her for a time, Dave and I were ready to tackle Hatcher Pass Road, a 49-mile strip of rugged gravel lined with breathtaking scenery. Elevation at the summit is 3,886 feet where, in July, patches of snow-covered tundra intermix with lush green foliage. We saw a beaver dam, a profusion of colorful alpine wildflowers, Alaskan cotton and, at lower elevations, fields of spectacular magenta fireweed.

From 1938 through 1941, the Alaska Pacific Consolidated Mine Company, a large gold producer, operated on a site near the summit. Now being restored, the 277 acres at the Independence Mine State Historical Park contain several old mining buildings and machinery.

A visitors' center in the former superintendent's house displays photos and artifacts of the mine during its active days. Winding southward toward Palmer, the Hatcher Pass Road parallels the rocky rapids of the Little Susitna River where a few independent gold claims are still being worked by persistent prospectors.

Salmon bake

On a return visit to Fairbanks, we met Kirk Dalton who taught us that the route to adventure can be complicated.

"I met this babe who asked me if I wanted to come to Alaska," said Kirk as he grilled slabs of delicious fresh salmon for us over an open fire at Alaskaland. "That was four years ago. I was 20 then. After a few months, the girl went back to her family. I stayed here. Later I went home and married Julie, my high school sweetheart.

"I'd been going to college in San Luis Obispo—studying to be an engineer before my first trip up here," Kirk explained. "I'd never seen snow. I lived in a tent that first year—until there was two feet of snow. Then I built a cabin. Dad had taught me all of the practical things so I just applied them. When I was 21, I built a house for Julie and me. Now I have my own business—refinishing and building furniture. That's one thing about living up here—you learn to be a multi-purpose person. You have to be."

In addition to his furniture business, Kirk operates the popular Salmon Bake concession at Alaskaland, a 44-acre

Kirk Dalton serves up grilled salmon at Alaskaland.

walk-through museum created near Fairbanks in 1967 as the Alaskan State Centennial Park to commemorate the 100th year of American sovereignty.

Kirk and his friends offer a smorgasbord salmon, halibut and rib dinner complete with baked beans, potato salad, home-baked rolls, relishes, dessert and beverage for a price competitive with fine restaurants.

Kirk shared his recipe for grilled salmon. "Mix equal parts of lemon juice, brown sugar and margarine. Heat. Baste just shortly before taking the fish off the fire." It was so delicious that we went back for dinner two nights in a row. I've used the recipe at home and it brings back memories.

"Alaska doesn't segregate people according to age or sex," Kirk said as he served us our second helping of salmon. "Once you develop a reputation for doing good work here, you'll never go hungry."

Besides his furniture business and cooking at Alaskaland, Kirk is a professional scuba diver. "People rely on one another for services," he explains. "We make enough money in the summer to get us through the winter—usually. In summer there's wood to cut, gardens to grow and food to preserve."

Alaskans depend on one another for survival as well as for services.

"I remember one night our car broke down," Kirk said. "Julie hadn't dressed properly for the 30 below weather. We sat there in our stalled car. We might have frozen to death, but a fellow whom we'd never met stopped his two-seated sports car and offered to take Julie home. Then he came back for me. When we arrived at his house, he handed me his car keys and told me to drive myself home and bring the car back when it was convenient. That's the way people are up here. You have to help one another to survive."

Ignoring the inconvenience of the cold, Kirk savors the adventure of Alaska and the sports that go with it. Besides scuba diving, he likes to look for whales, trap for furs and go cross-country skiing, hunting and fishing.

Julie, who doesn't share a love for all of Kirk's activities said, "Outdoors people who like to hunt and fish should come to Alaska. We have no canned entertainment here. We socialize, play cards, have dinner and refinish furniture during the cold weather."

Kirk said, "During the winter we stay in our own little cliques, relying on one another, for the winters are cold, dark and depressing."

"That first year we lived in a cabin with no windows," Julie said. "By February I was terrible to live with. People who are nice the rest of the year get cabin fever in the winter. Many men work on the North Slope and the women are left alone a lot. Or sometimes a couple may both work on the North Slope and take in $17 an hour apiece," says Julie. "It depends upon what you're doing there how much you make; but you can get even bigger money for overtime. Some people have made $40,000 in four months and drawn unemployment the rest of the year.

"Salaries are high here, but both partners in a marriage need to work to buy food, fuel and other necessities," added Julie who is secretary to the vice president of a bank. Julie likes her work, but she doesn't relish going to the office and coming home in the dark all winter. But that's the way it is in the Arctic. Julie would like to go back to her family and the sunshine in California, but she remains and adapts because she loves Kirk and knows he loves the life here.

Julie and Kirk are realistic about the problems facing couples in Alaska. If too much time is devoted to money making, the relationship may be threatened. "Sometimes it's the marriage *or* the money," Kirk said.

Of course that could be true anywhere, I thought.

The Pipeline

The pipeline is a shining, silvery snake, four feet in diameter and 800 miles long. Slithering through forests, across rivers and over tundra, it's a scar on the landscape in the eyes of environmentalists, a boon to the economy for many others.

The pipeline brought the workers. The workers came for jobs and money. The money which the oil brought in tax revenues has been dispersed now throughout the state to help build homes and businesses, develop resources, establish schools and pay teachers' salaries.

Money brought Lee to Alaska. After teaching for six years in Valdez, she was ready for a change. She quit her job, found a financial partner and began to speculate in land.

Operating out of a shop they've named "Serendipity," the two women sell jewelry and other tourist-type novelties and continue land speculation. It was at this shop that we met them on our first trip to Alaska.

"This is a melting pot—the last frontier," Lee said. "There's opportunity here in Alaska. People come here for money, adventure and elbow room. This is a cosmopolitan society, yet there's lots of space to move around."

Her partner added, "Alaska has the largest unemployment rate in the country, but that's because many people work at seasonal jobs."

The tourist trade is seasonal. The craft and gift shops sell mostly to travelers—like us—going to Valdez from Anchorage, but they also sell to pipeline workers who want to send jewelry or moccasins back to their families in the Lower 48 or in Anchorage.

Although Lee and her partner refer to themselves as environmentalists, it's the pipeline that provides income for them to live and to speculate. The two enterprising women enjoy the elbow room, but the investment opportunitites are equally attractive.

En route from Anchorage to Valdez we stopped at Worthington Glacier. As we carefully followed the path to get as close as possible to the blue ice, we met a young man climbing around on the crusty snow with his wife and two small children.

Chatting with them, we learned that the man had been working on the pipeline for six years. "We're a young family," he said. "We can't afford to look ahead too far at this point. Yes, I make good money on the pipeline. No, I don't like the work. Yes, it's good to be up here away from our families. We develop some independence although I think we miss some of our heritage by not being near the children's grandparents."

While tromping around the glacier, we also stopped to talk with a young woman traveling alone with her dog.

"I've burned my bridges," she said. "I was drawn here by some emotional magic. I don't know why. I guess I came to find myself." We learned she had been a model maker for Boeing Aircraft in Seattle. "I fell in love with Alaska after talking about it with friends," she said.

She quit her job, packed everything she owned in her

Toyota pick-up and now was headed for Cordova, hoping to get a summer cannery job where she could be near the sea and possibly watch humpback whales.

"I think Alaska is open, free and beautiful. I can't stand living in a city—even Seattle," she exclaimed. "People tell me I can get a position in my trade in Anchorage, but I don't want to live in the city. I'd rather work in a routine job in the country."

The town that rose again

Tall mountains rise on all sides of Valdez, surrounding a calendar-picture small boat harbor that beckons would-be fishermen and seafood eaters.

But a different city stands today near the site of the picturesque old fishing village that was devastated by an earthquake and tidal wave on Good Friday in 1964. The new city was carefully planned and rebuilt on safer ground four miles from the original location. By 1968 the last residents of the original Valdez had relocated to their new homes. Designed by professional city planners, the city is now a model for others.

When Valdez was selected as the terminus of the 800 mile long trans-Alaska pipeline, the fishing village boomed. The community continues to prosper but one could easily imagine what the city must have been like in the heydey of pipeline construction.

We had driven down to Valdez from Anchorage, stopping to sleep in our pick-up truck one night en route. To be able to camp in such isolation is one of the things I love about Alaska, and a late evening beach walk was one of the highlights of the trip for me.

After our arrival in Valdez, I took time to transcribe some notes in the room we had rented for a couple of days in a private home. (The motels were full.) As I was typing away,

Dave returned from a walk to announce he had bought some shrimp—right off a shrimp boat—for lunch.

"Wonderful!" I said. "But who's preparing them and where?"

"No problem," Dave told me. "I bought $5 worth of shrimp and when I told the girl who sold them to me that we didn't have anywhere to cook them, she offered to do that for me on the boat. She's fixing them right now."

After a quick stop at a grocery for a bottle of cocktail sauce, we hurried to the pier. Sure enough, boiling on a propane hotplate in the cabin of the boat were at least two pounds of beautiful pink prawns.

Our shrimp boat friends enjoy life at the terminus of the pipeline.

Our cook and hostess was the daughter of the shrimp boat's owners. "My boyfriend and I supply the labor. Mom provides the boat," she explained.

Life on a shrimp boat may sound glamorous, but after the first trip, I think it might be monotonous. I'd love to eat shrimp every day, but to live day and night on a tiny boat and cook in a two- by four-foot kitchen would be more adventure than I'd care for.

The shrimp, boiled in a large coffee can, were delicious, and we had a feast right on the boat. Our cook declined to join us, for after all, shrimp were no treat for her.

After our feast we left the small boat for a larger one and a cruise through Prince William Sound.

Although we usually study up on local attractions and find our own way, the only way to visit the frozen face of the enormous Columbia Glacier is by boat. We bought tickets for the tour and prepared to compete for space along the rail to photograph sea lions, otters, porpoises and perhaps whales.

Alaska is famous for spectacular glaciers and among the best known and most easily viewed is the 41-mile-long Columbia. Of 440 square miles of blue ice, only the lower 12 miles can be seen from the bay.

As we neared the glacier, a giant iceberg broke off from the ice wall with a resounding crack like a sonic boom, splashing with a roar into the frigid waters of the sound. Here we were able to see as well as hear icebergs fall and splash into the water leaving trails of mist behind them.

While we watched the glacier, we also eyed Mount Einstein and Mount Witherspoon's majestic peaks in the background. Each has an elevation of more than 11,000 feet and they were still covered with snow in the middle of July.

The cruise satisfied our desire to see the glacier, but it also whetted our appetite to seek out more sea life. However, it was time to return to Anchorage.

Interlude

After six weeks of meandering around Alaska we drove home to Michigan through Canada—stopping at Jasper and Banff National Parks. The trip was pleasant, but we were anxious to get home to our children and the rest of our families. However, we were already planning our winter trip north. We looked for parkas and warm winter boots designed to take us to climates expected to be 40 degrees below zero.

After I had decided upon a navy blue hooded parka, I nearly returned it. It's ridiculous to buy a coat just for Alaska, I reasoned. I was sure I wouldn't need such heavy clothing except at Prudhoe Bay. And I wasn't sure I cared to go that far north.

However, I knew that going to Prudhoe Bay was something Dave wanted to do. Prudhoe Bay is the northern terminus of the pipeline and with some encouragement from me, he would have have driven us there the summer before.

While I was debating whether or not to keep my arctic parka, the temperature dropped below zero in Michigan. I got out my new jacket and wore it several times. Now I had no option but to keep it so I decided that I might as well get my money's worth and go to Prudhoe Bay. It was settled.

In February we drove to Chicago, spent the night there and the next morning boarded a plane for Minneapolis. It was already 30 degrees below zero at the Twin Cities airport when we climbed aboard the Northwest Airlines DC-10 that would take us to Anchorage via Seattle. I wondered how much colder it could be on the edge of the Arctic ice pack.

Although we flew into a purple ribbon sunset, the fog was thick over Anchorage and we circled around the city for half an hour or more before the pilot finally announced an alternative landing—Fairbanks, 300 miles into the interior.

This detour, a serious inconvenience for some of the passengers, was a lark for us. No one was waiting for us in Anchorage; we were delighted with the extra sidetrip.

While some of our fellow passengers opted to take one of the small airlines back to Anchorage—despite the fog—we accepted the airline's offer to put us up overnight at the Captain Bartlett Inn.

The inn, a fifteen minute drive from the airport, proved to

be a quaint looking hotel. It could have come straight out of a movie. The stuffed game animals on the wall, the artist's easel in the lobby—all contributed to the frontier image.

The airline gave us vouchers for dinner and breakfast. While we waited for our shrimp salads to arrive, we listened to country music played by a black-bearded cowboy who tried to emulate Johnny Cash.

After our late dinner, we retired to our room where we learned that the central heating in the hotel has two settings—*on* and *off*. After the deep cold of Michigan and Minnesota, we were amazed to find that it was an unseasonably warm February evening in Fairbanks with the mercury up into the 30 degrees *above* zero, but it was at least 90 degrees in our room and the only thing we could do to get comfortable was to open the window wide.

One advantage of the climate here, however, was that the air was so dry that our cotton turtle necks, which we had hand washed, dried overnight.

Another surprise about this peculiar Alaskan winter was that after we settled ourselves in Anchorage the next day, rented a car and cross country skis, we couldn't find enough snow for skiing. We carried the rented skis around in the car for two days, but never found enough snow. Nevertheless, the winter landscape was as beautiful as it had been in summer. Icy waterfalls appeared on the sides of mountains and ice build-up on the water in the inlet was magnificent.

And then there were the Northern Lights. As we walked through a parking lot one evening on the way to our room, we chanced to glance up and saw lights swirling like ballerina skirts across the sky. Ribbons of mauve, blue, green and golden lights mingled and tangled directly above us. We'd read and heard about the *aurora borealis,* but we weren't prepared for such a show.

The Roughneck

Now that we had returned to Anchorage, we made arrangements to look up some people who were friends of friends. We had a long list of names, addresses and phone numbers. David Rhodes, who lived in Anchorage but worked at the north end of the pipeline at Prudhoe Bay, was one of them.

David Rhodes

David agreed to meet us at a restaurant near his home in Anchorage. Over a lasagna dinner, the red headed, mustached, slim, thirty-two-year old, six-foot-two man told us his story. He came to Alaska because there was a high-paying job for him in the oil fields.

"They call me a 'roughneck,'" he said. "This is strictly a blue collar job handling lengths of pipe and doing manual labor on the drilling floor."

Before coming to Alaska David had graduated from high school in southwestern Michigan, spent three years in th U. S. Army, worked as a fingerprint technician and later in a factory making automobile seatcovers.

"When they started laying off people at the shop where I was working, my brother and I went to look for jobs in Texas," David explained. "After six weeks, we were both hired by an oil drilling firm. I stayed in Texas learning my trade until '79 when I decided to come to Alaska."

David's experience on the Texas oil rigs helped him land a job in Prudhoe Bay with one of the companies who contract to drill for the major oil companies.

"Yes, it gets cold on the North Slope," David said. "The drill sites are on the shore of the Arctic Ocean where the mercury sometimes drops as low as 60 degrees below zero Farenheit with 50 miles per hour winds. I've been frostbitten on my wrists. To keep from freezing my hands, I always carry extra gloves. As soon as one pair gets wet, I put on a new pair. We pick up a fresh stack of gloves every day. If you grab metal with a wet glove, your glove stays there."

Unlike those in Texas, the drilling rigs at Prudhoe Bay are enclosed to keep out the fierce arctic weather. Winters are frigid along the edge of the polar ice cap, but David says he may work in a T-shirt during the short arctic summer when temperatures may soar to a scorching 70 degrees.

Oil drillers are paid well because their jobs are among the most dangerous on earth. One of the riskiest parts of David's job is to climb the snow ladder on the derrick—150 feet in the air—every day to grease the crown on the derrick.

"I'm also in charge of the 'mud' that lubricates the drilling bit and the pumps that force the viscous fluid down into the ground to seal the hole," he said.

David, like most of the men and women who share his dangerous occupation, is proud of his work on the North Slope. "We do directional drilling so that we don't tear up much of the tundra," he explained. "The rig is set on a gravel strip about the size of three football fields, but from each site we can angle the drill bits to tap several acres of underground oil reserves."

I decided that life in Alaska's arctic oil fields must consist of long hours of routine, hard, dangerous work punctuated by moments of excitement and discovery.

"My crew drilled a 'record' well last winter," David said, grinning proudly. "It took us only a little more than twelve days. But that isn't why I work here—to set records."

Nor is it only the money that attracts him although workers on the oil rigs earn as much as $80,000 a year. "There's a lot of competition for these high-paying jobs," David admitted.

Oil drillers' jobs are among the most dangerous in the world.

"On the Slope you have to have a pleasing personality as well as be a dependable worker. Only the best survive the intense competition and the grueling 84-hour weeks.

"Being a team person is very important. You can't be in a low mood every couple of days because each man on the crew depends upon everyone else, not only to do his job correctly and safely, but to help keep up morale."

David's drill site rises like a spacecraft launching pad, 150 feet above the barren arctic desert, 42 miles from the airport at Prudhoe Bay. He and 34 others live in quarters much like a complex of connected mobile homes. Residents share dining facilities where the food is plentiful and well prepared.

"We can have all we want to eat, and we can eat whenever we want," David told us.

To us, the Arctic seemed to be an entirely different world. "Time of day means nothing there," David said. "There's no daylight at all in the winter and there's no place to go." Most crews on the slope work 12 hour shifts for 7 or 14 days, and the workers spend their leisure hours sleeping, reading, playing cards and watching movies.

"The 34 of us in our camp have to share the two daily newspapers that are flown in, and there's no radio or TV. We're stagnant for two weeks as far as news goes."

Since he works two weeks and is off one week, that means David is home only one third of the time. We wondered how the unusual schedule affected his personal life.

"I worry about things going wrong while I'm gone," he said, "like the dishwasher vibrating or the electricity being wired up wrong."

David's wife Cheryl operates an electrolysis business in their suburban Anchorage home. David has adopted Cheryl's two children from a former marriage and works hard to make a good family life for them all. "After being gone two weeks, the first day back home is tough," David admitted. "I try to relax. We can't do all of the things we want to do in one week, but we've been remodeling our home and putting in a new fireplace."

"We look forward to the long days of summer," David said. "Then we can go camping and fishing, take naps, get up and eat some more. Our time together is great because it's in week-long blocks. We can really take advantage of some of Alaska's special opportunities.

"We see a lot of moose here," he said. "It's not uncommon to pass a moose on the way to the bank. I want to go bear hunting sometime. We already have a spot picked out for the rug.

"Contrary to what many Outsiders think, one still needs four seasons of clothing here—just like in Michigan," he added. "And food is expensive. But we save by buying thirty loaves of bread at a time and we purchase canned food by the case."

David Rhodes will probably remain in Alaska, I thought. His wife and family are here; he has a good job; and he's making good money. He's not likely to head back Outside—except to visit. But I don't think it's money that's holding him here. Alaska has become a way of life.

Woman of achievement

After talking with David Rhodes, my David was even more anxious to visit Prudhoe Bay. We met Becky Pfanner, senior representative of public affairs for Atlantic Richfield Company (ARCO), when we were exploring alternatives for visiting the oil fields.

As part of her job with ARCO, Becky works with the media and arranges tours of the company's facilities at Prudhoe Bay and other remote areas. She coordinates special events like the ARCO Jesse Owen games and supervises the company's 50-member Speakers' Bureau.

"Alaska is exciting, adventuresome, beautiful," Becky

said. "On the negative side, we're away from family. The winters are dark. Some people withdraw. But others get involved in the community, ski, and enjoy life in Alaska."

Becky is a petite brunette whose vivacious enthusiasm is contagious. When Becky is around, one can't be a pessimist or complain about anything. She doesn't stand for it. Her motto is: "There's opportunity here. Go get it!"

Becky, who has a journalism degree from Oregon State, arrived in Anchorage with her husband when he came to work with the public health service. Becky went to work at ARCO as a receptionist. Eleven months later she had been promoted to the public relations department. Now she has her own office overlooking the city of Anchorage. Her marriage terminated somewhere along the way.

Becky and her fiance U. S. Army Lieutenant Richard Parker took us out to dinner at the top of the Captain Cook Hotel where the four of us shared interesting conversation, a fabulous dinner and a breathtaking view of the city and the Inlet.

Over dinner, Becky was eager and willing to talk about Alaska and the opportunities it offers. During her seven years with ARCO Becky said she has seen the company make real progress in improving opportunities for women. "I've seen women move from secretarial jobs to technical and professional positions," she said. "There were no women working for ARCO on the North slope until 1976. Now there are more than 100."

But as one of Alaska's corporate women on the go, Becky didn't appear to be one who would stand still. I asked her about her plans for the future.

"I get anxious to go Outside sometimes, but it's always great to get back to Alaska. I don't plan to leave Alaska. I'm a career girl, but even if the opportunity came for me to move up in my work, I would turn it down if it meant moving to Los Angeles or Houston.

"I love Alaska," she stressed. "Anchorage is like a small

town even though it's the biggest city in the state. Everybody knows what's going on. After being out of town, I come back and while riding from the airport to my apartment, the taxi driver fills me in on what happened while I was away.

"If I go and sit in the little restaurant at the Captain Cook, dozens of people come by and wave and say, 'Hi, Becky!' That's important."

"There's an undefinable mystique about Alaska," said Lieutenant Richard Parker, who planned to leave the Army soon after seven years of service.

As we ate our salads, Richard told us his story.

"I was born in the village called North Pole so you see, I'm a native Alaskan. My parents live in Georgia now, but I've been stationed in Anchorage for three years.

"I have a teaching degree so maybe I'll teach here. I want to stay in Alaska because I enjoy the recreational aspects. As part of my military duty, I ran a fish camp where the soldiers would come for rest and recreation. I also like to ski."

Because he's an Alaskan with established residency, Richard should have priority finding a teaching job. There appear to be openings in the bush for people who are mobile and willing to teach anywhere.

But even if Richard insists on remaining in Anchorage, the fact that he's physically there will give him an advantage over other job candidates from Outside.

Again in Anchorage five years later, we called Becky. She was delighted to hear from us and insisted that we visit their new mountainside suburban home and have cherry pie and coffee with her and Richard. They had married and now had two children. Becky had been promoted at ARCO to be Director of Government and Community Relations for South Central Alaska.

Richard teaches physical education in a junior high school in Anchorage, and during the summer months works as a general contractor supervising building and painting.

Richard was putting finishing touches on the couple's

Richard Parker and Becky Pfanner Parker enjoy entertaining in their mountainside home near Anchorage.

elegant home. The spacious redwood structure with a solar greenhouse, winding staircase and contemporary Italian kitchen was designed especially for entertaining and features a balcony overlooking Cook Inlet. White gallery walls in the entrance hall set off Becky's collection of prints by two of her favorite artists.

Three-year-old Kathleen and two-year-old Garrett watched a video cassette of "The Wizard of Oz" while Becky prepared a snack for them.

"We had a live-in housekeeper and babysitter for a time," Becky explained. "But now we want to take care of the children ourselves."

Wearing a pink jogging suit and sitting on a plush beige sofa in her living room, the petite executive seemed relaxed, but radiated confidence and exuberance. Later as she wheeled a tea caddy into her living room, Becky seemed as poised as in her navy hopsack suit sitting behind her desk at ARCO.

"I have to keep up with government policies, but I spend my time in the community," she said. "I have a colleague who is a lobbyist." She and Richard had recently hosted a reception for gubernatorial candidates in their new home.

Becky would be good in politics. I asked whether she had political ambitions. "I'm learning about politics as I go," she said. "Maybe I'll have something to contribute. I know the politicians and I think I could do well in politics, but I'm on this other career path right now. Besides, I wouldn't want to take time away from my family."

Having worked for three different managements since she began, Becky has proven herself in the business world. At 36 she is successful and still climbing.

"Sure I miss spring in Oregon," she added. "But I know more than 5,000 Alaskans. I see these people at a lot of functions. And if Richard and I and the children want to get away as a family for the weekend, we can.

"I wouldn't like to live in an uninsulated cabin and buy my clothes at the thrift shop," Becky said. "I don't care about bush living, but I love Alaska."

Top of the world

It was Becky who helped us arrange to visit the oil fields along the shore of the Arctic Ocean. The North Slope in winter seems like the surface of the moon, except there's snow at Prudhoe Bay rather than moon dust. It was 10 a. m., still dark, and 41 below zero when our Wein Air Alaska jet touched down in the ice fog at Prudhoe Bay. But we were warmly welcomed at the airport.

Dana Stabenow, zipped snuggly into a blue quilted parka and corduroy slacks, was driving a carryall belonging to the Standard Oil Company of Ohio (SOHIO). Dana's blonde curly hair framed her friendly smile as we set out on a journalist's tour of SOHIO'S facilities.

The frozen flatland across the top of Alaska is a desert of snow during the long frigid winter. Because it was so cold we spent very few minutes outdoors—only long enough to go between our warm vehicle (Dana never shut off the motor) and the buildings and oil rigs. The Company's oilfield operations there encompassed an area 25 by 12 miles.

"The oil companies have worked on only 130,000 acres of tundra, out of nine million acres on the Slope," Dana explained. "When I first heard about this project, I thought the drillers would destroy the environment. But they haven't. I know that, if pushed, the big companies can run a successful and environmentally sound oil business. And they do. This is a special place. It's the first successful arctic production oil field in the world. Snow removal crews work twelve hours a day regularly. During storms, they work 24.

"We have three or four back-ups here for everything," she explained. "We're overly cautious. All of our vehicles contain radios. Whenever we go anywhere, we let someone know we're leaving and we tell the people at our destination that we're coming. We've never lost anyone in a storm yet."

Dana earned a degree in journalism from the University of Alaska and she had been on the slope five years. "I was hired as a clerk, worked for ten months and then was promoted to communications," she explained. "I'd had experience on a fishing boat and with an air taxi service. My parents were divorced when I was very young and my mother was a hand on a fishing boat."

At the time of our visit Dana was information services coordinator for SOHIO which means she gives several tours a week, writes and takes photographs for company publications and is Prudhoe Bay correspondent for the company's newsletter.

"I've matured a lot up here and have sharpened my interpersonal skills," Dana said. "SOHIO is my second family. You form friendships here that you wouldn't have time for otherwise. It's special working where no one ever worked before. We're proud of it, and we lie a little about the weather." (I didn't know whether she meant that they exaggerated the good or the bad points.)

"No, I don't go outdoors in the winter," she said, "except to get in and out of the truck when I go from station to station."

But there are plenty of recreational activities indoors. A swimming pool which also serves as an emergency fire fighting reservoir, table tennis equipment, pool table and volleyball court are available for employees' use. The recreation facilities are to be used between 6 a. m. and 10 a. m. and between 6 p. m. and 10 p. m. Other times are considered quiet hours. These people work twelve hour shifts, so when they return to their quarters, they need to relax and sleep.

If the oilfield workers' recreation is great, the food is better. The day we visited, the cafeteria offered a luncheon buffet of shrimp, oysters, ham, fresh fruit, tossed salad, beef stroganoff, coffee, tea, juice, milk and soft drinks. A smorgasbord is available around the clock, we were told. Employees and visitors eat whatever they want, whenever they want and as much as they want.

The decor is colorful and attractive—designed especially to keep people from getting cabin fever. Rooms are shared with a counterpart who is on the shift the opposite week. Personnel rotate weekly. Two individuals share a bath and lavatory, but each person has a bedroom with compact storage space, desk and bunk. Space is designed so that individuals can keep their belongings in the room while back home for the week. Thus they don't have to carry clothing and personal items back and forth on the plane.

"Everyone is equal where housing is concerned," Dana said. "There's no discrimination or rank among employees." To protect the tundra from thawing, buildings are erected on pilings above five feet of gravel which is set over twelve inches of tundra and over 2,000 feet of permafrost.

"Big trucks with balloon-like tires travel over the tundra without affecting it," Dana explained. "In fact, we've been told that they can even drive over people without hurting them. We've had no volunteers to test this theory, however."

Dana Stabenow works at the Top of the World. Mile "0" of the trans-Alaska pipeline is in the background.

We wondered about the mental health of the workers in general.

"To survive in a remote place, you need a sense of humor and an ability to get along with others," Dana said. "Our company gives psychological tests to would-be employees."

"The commute back to Anchorage is a minor detail," she said when I asked about it. "After all, it's only an hour and a half away. We all work twelve hour shifts, seven days a week. We ignore holidays. Holidays mean nothing unless you happen to have that week off."

Each oil company pays round trip transportation costs for its own workers—another reason for the attraction of Prudhoe Bay. Indeed, as we had thought, money was the chief drawing card.

As we toured the facility, Dana introduced us to several workers.

"Money—that's why we're here," said Jerry Parkinson, production controller at Prudhoe Bay. Jerry's home is in the fishing country and mild climate of the Kenai Peninsula in southern Alaska. He came originally from Indiana.

We asked Jerry what is was like to be away from home half of the time.

"Trust is important," he said. "This is my second marriage. My wife has many friends and does a lot of activities on her own with folks from her church. I never see some of her friends or our neighbors. My contact with friends depends on my work schedule. I'm working a week and then I'm off a week. After I first came up here, I went home and taught my wife everything they taught us here about first aid and survival, so I know she's independent.

"Working on the slope is a whole different lifestyle; money is why we're here," Jerry repeated. "We can make twice as much here as we could in the Lower 48."

Texan George Carter is a also a production controller. "This is my second marriage too," he said. "My second wife knew what it would be like to have me work one week on and one week off. To keep herself occupied, she takes community education classes when I'm gone."

Larry Brott, another Texan, is an instrumentation technician responsible for controlling the flow of oil simultaneously from several wells. We asked him how one applies for such a specialized job.

"I just happened to have exactly the right skills for this job because of my former work experience," Larry said. "I applied for this job and I got it." That seems to be the key to employment in Alaska—or anywhere for that matter. If you have the needed skills, you can get a job. Keeping that job is up to you from then on, but having skills and experience opens the door.

Our return flight across the tundra and the Brooks Range brought us back to Anchorage the same day, but we had seen and learned a lot in a few hours at one of the most remote working sites on Earth.

Anchorage Again

Elevation 92 had been recommended to us as one of Anchorage's most exclusive seafood restaurants. When we went to have dinner there, we met Debbie Greenwald, a 22 year-old blonde hostess. Her ankle length red skirt swished as she showed us to a table overlooking Cook Inlet. During the day Debbie is an assistant producer for one of the three Anchorage TV stations.

Debbie had been a photojournalism major at Cleveland State University in Ohio. She said, "In the summer of 1980 I came up to Alaska as a tourist. My friend and I traveled all over Alaska; then I went back to school in Cleveland.

"When I came up again last summer, I knew I had to work and save money for school. I went around to all the places I was interested in and had interviews. When I was offered the job at the TV station, I couldn't turn it down, so here I am.

"Alaska is the most dynamic and exciting place to be right now. So I decided to take a year off from college and come here to get the experience in TV that I needed.

"There are all kinds of business opportunities in Alaska for people who use their imagination," she said. "My boy friend is 23 and he's the president of his own company called 'Green Connection.' He furnishes live plants for the restaurant and for many other businesses in town. Business is very good.

"We need a good bakery here," she added.

Air Force wife

As a member of the National Federation of Press Women (NFPW), I immediately began to look up Press Women when we arrived in Anchorage. *The Anchorage Times* seemed a logical place to start.

The first Press Woman I met was Nancy Schmitt, Lifestyle editor for the Times. She had just been promoted and was very busy, but she took time out to plan a luncheon meeting for Dave and me with several other Press Women.

The luncheon was a pleasant experience, but the day we ate lunch alone with Nancy at the Tea Leaf, she opened up. "Alaskans cope by reaching out to one another," Nancy told us as we waited for our egg drop soup one winter afternoon.

The Tea Leaf, a dimly lit Chinese restaurant, quickly became a favorite of ours for dining and interviewing. Located in the Sunshine Mall in downtown Anchorage, the bright yellow structure looked out over a vast parking lot built on land reclaimed after the great earthquake of 1964. By 1986 the Tea Leaf had moved to a more prestigious location across the street from the Anchorage Hilton.

"People share and lean on each other here in Alaska" Nancy explained. "People who work on the North Slope need support groups. The people you work with become your family. Your neighbors become your family. Frontier survival dictates that you can go into another isolated cabin for food and shelter." A number of people have built cabins in the bush that they use only occasionally. Other travelers are welcome to use them.

In Alaska, there are hundreds of military families. Some of the men, Nancy told us, really do enjoy the environment. They hunt and fish and take advantage of the opportunity. But sadly, many of their wives do not.

"Too many military wives make green ware ceramics and stay inside their apartments with their babies," Nancy said.

Nancy had been a military wife herself, but she, unlike many of the others, had looked for and found a job. She started as a reporter making $18,000 and afer five years was earning $27,500 as the TV and Lifestyle editor.

Her husband had just left the Air Force and was unemployed at the time. "He left because he didn't want to be transferred to Great Falls, Montana," Nancy explained.

The couple, originally from North Carolina, want to stay in Alaska, but there are frustrations. Nancy described how she was affected by cabin fever. "You can drive to Palmer. You can drive to Homer. You can drive to Seward. You can drive to Fairbanks. But it's always the end of the road. You can't get Out unless you have the money to spend on an airplane ticket." ("Out" is anywhere outside Alaska.)

Could the Schmitts make it on Nancy's salary? Would they be able to afford occasional travel?

"We could survive if we didn't have any debts," she explained. "But with the payments we have to make on various things, we keep getting farther and farther behind."

As we wandered around Alaska, Dave and I continued to think about seeking jobs in Alaska and moving there. What Nancy said about feeling trapped was something we had to consider. If we were to move to Alaska, we knew we'd have to leave many things behind. We'd need very lucrative jobs if we were to satisfy our desire to fly in and out of the state regularly.

After our meal at the Tea Leaf, with our head full of these thoughts, we wandered into an antique shop in Sunset Mall.

"People are different here," said a clerk in the shop. The

woman, whom we judged to be about 50 or so, added, "The average age here is 26, but no one pays any attention to how old you are. It's what you can do that counts. And people will assume you can do most anything. People leave their extended families when they come to Alaska and here they pick up new families. I'm a substitute grandmother right now for the little girl who lives next door to me."

In our trek around Alaska, we continually found that one of the reasons people come to The Great Land is for a change of environment.

"People change jobs constantly—like every two years or so," added the clerk. "There's no stigma to changing jobs. People assume that you're always looking for new opportunities. And people are willing to take risks here."

Never too old

When we checked out another Anchorage mall, we found Phil Richardson wearing a white chef's hat and blue and white striped denim apron. He was ladling hot fireweed jelly into sterile jars, whistling as he worked. In a few days he would celebrate his 75th birthday.

"These are the golden years," he said. "Many folks quit at my age, but God didn't make men to stop working when they reach old age. I believe folks should keep going until they drop in their tracks."

Phil was making use of the fruits of the land to earn a retirement living. The name of his small company was Raven Pond Jellies and we had sought him out because we wanted to purchase some of his products to take home as gifts. Phil had such a tremendous variety that we bought a dozen jars of jelly, including high and low bush cranberry, blueberry and fireweed.

After sampling wild berry jerky, a dried snack similar to

Phil Richardson has no plans to retire.

beef jerky, we purchased a dozen packets of that too. It would be ideal for backpacking and camping, we decided. It was non-perishable, lightweight and would provide quick energy.

We were interested in the products Phil had to offer but found him even more interesting as he told us his story. "After getting out of the Army, I sold women's hosiery for 37 years on the west coast," Phil said. "Then I figured it was time to move on.

"At age 62, I knew my company would like to have me out of their hair, but I knew that when I left the company I would have to get into something else and probably would have to adjust to a different standard of living.

"I thought my wife and I should go where life was just beginning and bring our teenage children with us. So we sold our house and came to Alaska in 1968. My wife, who'd had experience in retail sales, went to work for a well known company and later for another company who appreciated her talents more. I worked for a men's store. I was too old to work on the pipeline. Our children went Outside, but they came back.

"The land office leased us 40 acres near Talkeetna at $125 a year. We have it for 55 years with an option for renewal. We had a cabin there and the countryside was covered with wild berries. Gradually we learned what could be done with the berries, and it came to me that maybe I could sell them. I called on a few store owners; they said they'd buy my jam and jelly if they met government requirements.

"So I started my own business. That was eleven years ago. Last year we increased our sales 37%. We'll continue to do more business, but I won't have to increase the size of my kitchen. I can do more volume by selling retail, but we'll keep a few of the best wholesale accounts."

Phil had just moved his production and marketing operation from Talkeetna to Anchorage. We watched as he screwed lids onto jelly jars and then stood back and admired his work.

"I always feel like I've got just one more good job in me," Phil said. "That's what my dad used to say. I used to go backpacking and jogging but I can't walk and carry the stuff now. My arteries are 90% closed. But that doesn't affect my working here."

Teaching in Alaska

"There's plenty of opportunity in Alaska," exclaimed Stowell Johnstone, assistant superintendent of the Anchorage school system, "far more than in the Lower 48."

Stowell, who had been an Air Force reserve colonel as well as a school administrator, looked the part. He had come into the country as an English teacher fifteen years ealier. He had grown up in Idaho. He and his wife, who is in real estate, have four children—now in their twenties.

One daughter teaches special education during the school year and works in a print shop in the summer. Another is employed in layout at the *Anchorage Daily News*. One son is on the North Slope as a mechanic for one of the contractors. The other son, according to Dad, is "a ski bum" who has various enterprising things going.

"Our children have started forming friendships only with people whom they believe will remain in Alaska," Stowell said. "They've found that having friends move away is too traumatic."

We had looked up Stowell because he and Dave had met in Colorado a couple of years earlier at an Air Force conference. Because Dave and I had both been teachers, we were particularly interested in what he had to say about teaching in Alaska.

Speaking as an administrator, Stowell said, "The teachers' union is the most powerful group in Alaska. They're a rather stable group."

He explained that there are many applicants for every teaching job in Anchorage, and that for people really looking for a job here, their best bet is willingness to be assigned to a remote village bush school.

Stowell was planning to retire from the school system that summer and wasn't sure what he'd do next. He said he had several options. "I might go to work for an oil company, but then entertaining customers would be part of the job and I'm not sure I want to be that committed."

Another possibility would be to spend more time at his favorite fishing place on the Kenai River. "We started out with a small trailer at the fishing camp; then we got a larger trailer with a bedroom and added a lean-to for guests," he said.

"People could make it financially here on ten percent more than they made in Seattle and not change their lifestyle," he said. "Trouble is, most folks up here play more than folks do in the Lower 48. They eat out most of the time and spend money like crazy."

Questioned about the future of Anchorage, Stowell predicted, "Anchorage may grow into another Houston. That won't necessarily destroy it, but it will change it. People who want to live in the bush will just have to move farther out."

We were saddened to hear this, but we weren't surprised. We realized that frontiers disappear and the best one can hope is that there will always be one more frontier. At present, there's room to move back further into the bush. But for how long, we wondered?

Dave and I thought about the possibilities for teaching in Alaska. We recalled having met another teacher while we were in Eagle.

When we first saw her, Jan Dieters was walking along the unpaved main street of the isolated river town of Eagle wearing a yellow hooded rain slicker, chatting with a young student. A collie dog trotted along beside her.

Jan, we learned later, had grown up in Chicago and graduated from Northern Michigan University in Marquette in the upper peninsula of Michigan. She had taught special education in Anchorage for four years.

"Special education teachers burn out quickly," Jan had explained. "Teaching mentally impaired students was very intense for me, so I took a year off and lived in a one-room cabin on the Forty-Mile River where I did some gold mining."

Then she got a job teaching in Eagle. When we saw her there, she looked the picture of health and enthusiasm. There were only seven students in Jan's combined grade one, two and three classroom. She loved her work but admitted that social life in Eagle wasn't all that great. She said she would probably apply somewhere else, for a 29 year-old single girl just doesn't have many dates in Eagle.

We'd been eager to meet anyone in Alaska who would talk with us, but we were especially pleased to learn that Jan's sister-in-law had been a student in the school in Lakeview, Michigan when I was teaching there twenty years before. That student was now Rita Dieters who was living in Kodiak. Friends in Lakeview had told us to be sure to look up Rita.

Kodiak Island

After many phone calls via the Kodiak school superintendent's secretary who contacted Rita Dieters by radio at the family's fishing site, we were able to talk directly with Rita and she agreed to meet us at the Kodiak airport.

Although Rita didn't remember me at first, I still pictured her as the pretty little red haired seventh grader wearing blue shorts and a white shirt in a gym class in the school where I'd taught.

"When I got off the ferry in Kodiak nine years ago, it was foggy and rainy and I was crying," Rita told us. "But the sun came out, and we've stayed nine years."

When Rita and David Dieters were finishing the course work for their teaching degrees at Michigan State University, David said, "Let's do something really crazy—like going far away to teach for a year."

Rita agreed and after writing a number of letters, they landed an interview in Chicago with a school administrator from Kodiak who hired them on the spot. My Dave and I loved Kodiak the moment we arrived and could certainly see why the Dieters had remained on the island.

Rita grew up in a rural area of central Michigan. David was

city bred—a native of Chicago. Driving one hour to work and one hour back each day on an expressway was hardly his idea of adventure, so a chance to teach on Kodiak Island, which is accessible only by air or boat, seemed like the opportunity for which he had been looking.

When they settled in Kodiak, Rita taught first grade at the Coast Guard Base School on the island; and David taught at one of the city's elementary schools. David continued teaching and coaching, but after five years in the classroom, Rita took time out to have a family. It was at Rita and David's home that we met five-year-old Darrin, two-year-old Janelle and a new arrival less than three months old.

The Outsider's typical image of Alaska is wilderness, but Rita and David live within the city of Kodiak where Rita has a garbage disposal and microwave oven in her kitchen and thick carpeting and a plush sectional sofa in the living room. The couple remodeled a historic sea captain's home for their family's comfort and convenience.

"Living in a warm, pleasant place helps keep away cabin fever during long winter nights," Rita said. "Kodiak is one of the most beautiful spots in Alaska. The summers are gorgeous, but David goes to work and comes home in the dark in the wintertime. So our home is very important to us. When some of the people on the island start to feel cooped up, they either drink too much or relieve their tensions by going to Anchorage or Outside."

But Rita feels the long, dark winters have strengthened instead of strained the fabric of her family. She and David spend a lot more time with their children.

"Our kids get to know us," she explained. "We read a lot and communicate with our children. I want my kids to have warm feelings and the kind of closeness with us that I remember having with my parents."

That's the one thing Rita said that she dislikes about Alaska—her parents are too far away. Her parents do get to Kodiak for regular visits, and Rita goes back Outside with the children once a year. But the time between visits seems too long.

Outsiders think of Alaska as the land of ice and snow, but Rita said, "Yes, the streets are often icy, but we usually have to shovel our driveway only once a season. Our weather here in Southern Alaska is warmer and milder than it is in Michigan. Sometimes we wish there were more snow—so we could go cross country skiing more often."

Rita said most people in Kodiak own a pick-up truck and a boat rather than a second car, and they spend a great deal of time hunting and fishing. Rita's sister and brother-in-law had just driven a new pick-up truck from Michigan for Rita and David. Rita and David then paid their plane fare back to the Lower 48 after a couple weeks of visiting.

"We wanted the pick-up and it was less expensive to purchase it in Michigan," Rita explained.

When we asked about the natives on Kodiak Island, Rita said, "The natives are Aleuts. Many go to school Outside but few finish school because Aleuts tend to be shy, quiet people who often feel uncomfortable in a big city like Seattle. So they come home to stay."

Rita and David share the natives' attachment to the soft green island surrounded by some of the world's finest fishing. David soon took up commercial gill net fishing; now he and Rita spend their summers on the beach at Moser Bay on the southern part of Kodiak Island—about 45 minutes from the city by float plane.

Here at their remote fish camp on the bay, the Dieters net red salmon, pink salmon and dog salmon. But there are few of the conveniences of home. There's no telephone in their 12 x 12-foot cabin. Urgent messages are broadcast by a local radio station service called The Crabber Network or delivered by the tender boat that arrives twice daily at the camp to haul their catch to the cannery. Non-urgent messages simply aren't sent.

Rita said, "We were lucky. We bought our strip of shoreline when it was still possible to get a fishing lease for $1. Leases now may cost as much as $65,000—if you can get someone to sell one. It's like trying to buy a taxicab license in New York City."

Fishing fits perfectly into David Dieter's teaching schedule. In his spare time in March, he builds and repairs the boats. In April he readies and hangs the nets. Then he and Rita work at the fish site all summer.

Photo courtesy of Dieters

For David and Rita Dieters commercial salmon fishing provides a good life as well as good income.

Rita explained, "Gill net fishing is stationary. We catch the fish at Moser Bay and put them in our holding boat until the tender comes by to pick them up. We believe that our gill net salmon are a better quality than seine fish because ours are still alive when they reach the cannery."

Operators of each tender are required by law to report to the canneries how many fish they have on board, and the canneries report to the State Fish and Game officials who monitor the number taken and determine when fishermen may put out their nets. Although some Alaskan fishermen oppose State regulation, Rita said controls are necessary.

"There are those would would come out 365 days a year, put out their nets and catch everything that swims," Rita said.

"Close government supervision and industry cooperation ensure a consistent supply of fish. If too many salmon are taken, not enough will survive to spawn, and the future supply of fish will be threatened."

Roughing it in the fish camp at Moser Bay has some fringe benefits, we learned. "I don't have to go grocery shopping all summer," Rita said. "I order everything in advance and have it sent out on the tender."

Rita and David preserve the salmon they keep for themselves in a stainless steel canner over an apartment size propane gas stove. On open shelves in the kitchen corner of their cabin are a jar of instant Nestea, powdered milk, cocoa mix, pancake mix, packages of dried foods and a neat row of coffee mugs and stacks of glass and pottery bowls. Outside the cabin, a motor, paddles and fishing gear share beach space with Darrin's and Janelle's toys.

"On days when commercial fishing isn't allowed, we're permitted to set up a small subsistence net to catch fish which we smoke, can or pickle for our own use and give as gifts to friends and relatives," Rita explained.

To make canning easier at the cabin, Rita has both propane and oil stoves. "We even have hot running water," Rita said.

Hunting is good in season, and the human residents share the island with Kodiak brown bears, the world's largest carnivores. One night at Moser Bay Rita heard the dogs howling. The next morning she saw a bear trail directly behind their cabin.

"It's scary sometimes, but there are compensations—like having time for arts and crafts," Rita said. "We take handicraft projects to the cabin—because occasionally there is lots of time with nothing to do—especially on 'no fishing' days when there are no fish to preserve."

Rita explained, "Every summer we take a teen-age helper to the cabin. This can be either a boy or a girl, but the person must be a good reader. We don't want someone around who has to be entertained when there isn't work to be done. It's two miles down the beach to the next cabin, and there aren't any other teen-agers around. Our helpers have to provide their own entertainment. Since we have no electricity at the camp, they often bring a battery operated radio or cassette player."

If the helper is a girl, she often babysits while Rita works on the boat picking fish from the nets. If the helper is a boy, he spends more time working on the nets and Rita does more of the babysitting.

"But we all share the chores," Rita said. "I help with the fishing and Dave helps with the work in the cabin—like canning salmon." Work at the fish site also includes untangling kelp from the net and removing crabs, bullheads and starfish that collect along the lead line.

"If kelp is allowed to dry in the net, it becomes like wire," Rita explains. "We also have holes to mend on the days we're not allowed to fish. Seals and sea lions occasionally foul up our gear," Rita added. "We have a permit to shoot the animals if necessary, but they're legally protected and people are fined heavily for keeping pelts and ivory."

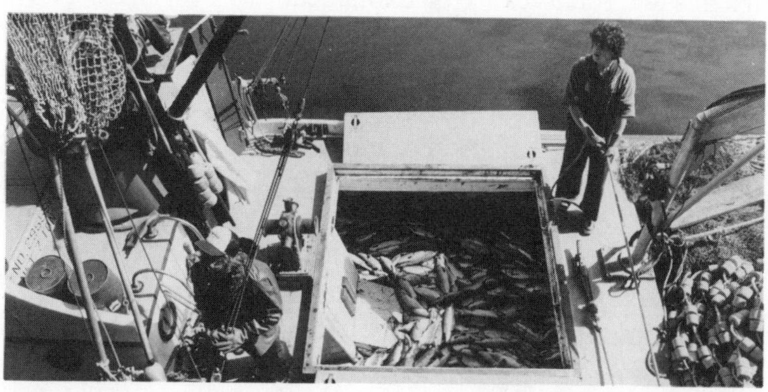

A fish tender hauls Dieters' catch into Kodiak for processing.

Kodiak Island, like much of Alaska, is a fisherman's paradise. "The fish market here in Kodiak went out of business," Rita said. "People here could catch their own fish—or barter for them. They didn't need to buy fish at the market."

It's important for their budget that the family preserve their own fish for their own use, Rita told us. "If I were to go to the store here in Kodiak to buy a tin of salmon, it would cost me the same as it would cost you in Michigan."

Some of the salmon is labeled Outside, but most of the salmon caught in Alaska is processed in Kodiak. The island is noted for its 22 canneries where most of the world's supply is canned or frozen; the town's pride is salmon although the canneries also process crab and shrimp.

"Most of the people in Kodiak are either cannery employees, fishermen, teachers or military personnel." Rita said.

"Kodiak is a beautiful place, but you either like it or you don't," Rita remarked. "It's important to have hobbies and interesting activities. The long dark winters are blamed for some of our problems—like the high divorce rate. Many people—both men and women—become alcoholics. There's only one movie theater in town so many people pay $40 a month to watch cable TV."

Rita Dieters and daughter Janelle blend into the Kodiak landscape.

But Rita and David have found plenty of things to do.

"Before we had a family, Dave and I coached athletic teams at school," Rita said. "We traveled with the teams, and that can be an ordeal in Alaska. First David had to obtain a special license to drive the school bus. Then we'd take the teams on the ferry and sleep overnight in sleeping bags in school gyms with the kids. We would usually be on the road for ten days with 18 teen-agers, and then there was also the possibility that the team might get snowed-in or fogged-in en route."

But in spite of the traveling hassles, Rita seemed to thrive on the activity. "Our athletic teams are good," she said. When Rita was coaching the girls' cross country team, Kodiak earned three state championships.

David has taken courses at the community college on how to mend nets, how to build aluminum boats and how to climb mountains. His latest course is carpentry.

Rita added, "Although I like not being around so many people much of the time, I do make occasional trips to Anchorage where I give my charge card a good workout."

Another outing the couple enjoys is to take off in their car, pick-up or boat and look for cedar driftwood on the beaches. This not only is entertainment but helps save on fuel costs.

"There are few restrictions on camping," Rita said, "and Dave can sport fish most anywhere and go moose hunting in season. He's teaching our kids to hunt and fish, and we want to raise our kids in a place where they can go for a walk." They hope their children will love Alaska as much as they do.

Teachers talk

Rita is a great organizer and hostess. When asked if she could set up some interviews for us, she drove us to meet Bill and Ann Barker.

Here we found an ultra modern new home with open spaces—designed by Ann, an art major, and built by the two of them with the help of friends and relatives. A woodburning stove was a focal point in the family living area and a spotlessly white kitchen attracted our attention. Artistic touches such as woven pillow covers and hand crafted wall hangings gave a lived-in look.

After graduating with the class of '58 in Colon, a small town in southern Michigan known as the Magic Capital of the World, Bill joined the U. S. Army.

"The Army shipped me to Fort Richardson, an army base located about eight miles outside of Anchorage, in 1960," he explained. Bill served two years at Fort Rich, then his tour of duty was up.

"The Federal Aviation Agency hired me to help with land surveys although I'd had no experience in surveying," Bill related. "I was what they call a rod man and worked with the surveyors all over Alaska—in King Salmon, Bethel, Dillingham, Cordova and Juneau."

Dave and I had been to Juneau. The other names are places on the map where the roads don't go. We begged him to continue.

"In the fall of '62 I went home and enrolled at Michigan State University where I met Ann," Bill said.

But memories of Alaska drew Bill back in the summer of '63. This time he attended the University of Alaska at Fairbanks, worked at the state department of aviation from January to October in '64 and then went back home and looked up Ann who by that time had finished her degree at MSU and was working in Detroit.

"As part of our marriage contract, Ann and I agreed we'd come to Alaska. She finished her master's degree. We had both been working. We had $7,000 and our car was paid for. I'd seen lots of people in miserable financial condition here so I was glad we weren't coming empty handed."

After a few false starts both of them were employed in

Alaska. Ann taught painting at the Community College in Kodiak and Bill landed a job in vocational education but needed a degree to keep the job. So although they had already bought a house and a fish site near Kodiak, they went back Outside where Bill finished his degree and Ann worked in a women's resource center.

Since they returned to Alaska, Bill has been teaching and Ann has started a volunteer crisis rap group on the island. Ann also paints, weaves and works at the fishing site.

"Fishing is our main income," she said. "Weaving and painting are expensive. I couldn't do those projects and we couldn't buy cars or have this home it if weren't for the fishing. Bill makes a good salary teaching—nearly twice as much as he would make back in the Lower 48, but we couldn't live on the salary. We could exist—but not *live*."

Fishing allows the Barkers a higher standard of living.

Ann and Bill Barker and their children enjoy their modern home on Kodiak Island.

"Fishing is our life and we love it," Ann said. Their two junior high school aged children work with them helping to build boats and hang nets.

"When the women started coming and helping at fish camp, we had to build an outhouse and put in a shower," Bill said. They get their water from a hose in the creek and heat it with a coil in the stove.

Although Alaska was in the Barkers' plans for a long time, Ann told us, "Part of the story is the fear of going back Outside and admitting we didn't make it. The first four years we were unsuccessful fishing, but we kept at it. Eventually the fishing paid off. Bill has always been lucky.

"I was always a quiet person, but I like the out-of-doors," Ann said. "Now I'm doing things I'd never visualized myself doing. I'm even learning to fly an airplane.

"There's a mystique about Alaska," she added. "Here, we find self-satisfaction. We're able to have an impact. I feel needed. Here we can make things happen."

Ann's work with the women's volunteer crisis group had led to their plan to build a shelter for battered and sexually assaulted women. Three full time and five part time people were working in the program when we talked with Ann and Bill.

"Alaskans do a lot of things themselves rather than hiring it done," Ann added. She did much of the electrical work on their home, and they imported a relative from outside to do the plumbing.

"We could afford to fly 'our plumber' up here, take care of him and pay him Michigan wages," Bill said. "We saved ourselves money and he got a trip out of it, too."

Bill summed up his feelings about Alaska. "I'm jealously protective of Alaska. I want my friends to locate here, but not other people's friends."

When we last talked with Barkers, they were planning a trip around the continental United States and were going to teach their children by correspondence while they traveled.

Rita Dieters also introduced us to Tom and Kathy Wischer in Kodiak.

"We packed up and came to Alaska with no jobs," said Tom. "I had written to several communities two years earlier but had received no positive response so we just came and traveled the road. We're both teachers so we went to district offices and filled out applications all summer.

"My fascination with the North started when I was in the sixth grade reading in the library about pioneers, trappers and Indian fighters," he said. "I grew up in Wyandotte near Detroit, but when I went to Western Michigan University in Kalamazoo, I had more access to open country and farm land.

"Then I went back to Detroit and taught during the race riots and transition period. Meanwhile, Kathy was teaching in West Bloomfield.She was sponsoring the ski club there and when I went along to help chaperone, I realized West Bloomfield and the inner city were two different worlds. I felt I needed to move to the inner city myself to be effective there and I wasn't willing to do that. It was then we decided to make the move to Alaska.

"We spent some time at Russian River on the Kenai Peninsula. One day we drove to Soldotna and stopped at the school office. While we were there, the superintendent of Kodiak schools called the school office and said they had some openings on the island.

"For $33 each we flew from Homer to Kodiak," Tom explained. "Thus far I'd had an offer in Anchorage to be a cook in a sheep camp. Kathy would have gone back to the lower 48 had I taken that job.

"But we got off the airplane in Kodiak with knapsacks on our backs, took the bus to the school and had interviews with the principal. We hitchiked to Abercrombie Park, found a place to camp, pitched our tent in sunshine at 70 degrees in early August and dozed in the sun.

"The next day it rained," Tom continued. "We hitchhiked again and his time got permission to stay near the air terminal. We ended up sleeping in a bunkhouse where cannery workers stayed. There were empty crates, a Coleman stove and some bunks. We crawled into a bunk and fell asleep. Some fellows came in about 3 a. m., checked to see who we were, seemed to think we were 'Charlie and his girl,' went to bed and left again before we were up the next morning.

"The next day we went to Elmendorf Air Force Base and waited for phone calls from places where we had applied for jobs," Kathy added. "After Tom was hired at Kodiak, we flew home. Tom returned and stayed in a trailer with another family for six weeks. When I got a permanent job doing substitute teaching in Kodiak, I followed him." Tom has continued to teach and was principal at Kodiak High School when we met him.

"Being in Kodiak was like living our dreams," Kathy continued. "Alaska is a vast country. We had traveled in the Western United States and liked it, but Alaska is different. You don't have the feeling that you can get back into civilization easily."

"We flew, camped and beachcombed," Tom explained. "We had to make an attitude adjustment. When we lived in Michigan and I wanted to go pheasant hunting in Iowa, the license cost $8. I didn't go because I thought it cost too much. Here bush taxi service may cost $150 an hour. We pay it."

Kathy said, "We decided we were going to do everything we could. We have different priorities here. This land requires risk taking. You have to want to know how to be self sufficient. That's the key. You must be adaptable. There's a six-month deer season with a five deer limit. King crab and halibut are for the taking. We bought a boat and a motor and trapped beaver, fox and otter. I started tanning hides. I've learned a lot—including survival skills.

"We've also learned that you don't throw things away. You keep old things for parts, recycle them and use them

Tom and Kathy Wischer "like living our dreams."

again. You don't have the services here that you do in the Lower 48. You begin to do things yourself and find you have to become more self sufficient."

Kathy said that many people miss having a variety of stores at their disposal and that leads to a failure to adjust to Alaska. "You have to learn to use catalogs," she said. "And remember, it's dark in winter. It's cold and rainy. You get cabin fever. You have to create your own avocation. Many of the women here are taking aerobic dancing this winter—just like folks do Outside."

Kathy added, "There's no readily identifiable class structure in Alaska. You can't tell the wealthy from anyone else for they don't necessarily wear expensive clothing or have elaborate housing."

Tom and Kathy were a typical independent couple. It's the self-motivated people who come to Alaska, we decided. But Kathy stressed, "Knowing somebody here is important. And if somebody goes back Outside and talks about Alaska, it encourages others to come up and look for jobs."

"Most who come, stay," Tom said. "Alaska has a viable economy. There are more opportunities here. You have a better chance of being judged on your performance."

Like the Barkers, the Wischers have done well financially and, also like the Barkers, money wasn't their motivation. Kathy was a substitute teacher two years, secretary to the president of an airline two years, worked with the career education program at the high school four years and taught business education one year. Now she teaches business education at the community college part time. The couple's young son Adam was three months old when we talked with them.

The Wischers, like many others on Kodiak Island, fish in season at their site close to town. "We started fishing because of the lifestyle," Tom said, "and we built a cabin to use for fishing and hunting." The unit consists of a main cabin, a banya (sauna), an outhouse and smokehouse.

"Fishing provides a psychological balance for us," Kathy said.

"The immediate gratification out there at the fishing site is good," Tom added. "In teaching, the results aren't so readily seen, if ever."

Having both been teachers, Dave and I could identify with that. Have the Wischers found what they were seeking? I think so. They sought diversity, adventure, a new life. For Tom, it wasn't necessary to change his profession. He's doing here essentially what he might have been doing Outside, but he has the bonus of fishing, flying, camping, hiking and traveling. All this, and in addition, they've learned survival skills that would be an advantage for anyone anywhere.

But the bottom line seems to be that they're enjoying life.

Rita set up an appointment for us with John and Tina Witteveen in John's school office. Both John and Tina grew up in Holland, Michigan. After graduating from Western

Michigan University and teaching in Grand Rapids for six years, John came to teach on Kodiak Island.

"We had visited Tom and Kathy in Alaska during the summer of '73," John told us. "When a friend called and said there was a teaching position available here, we had a garage sale before I even had the interview."

John is the assistant superintendent in Kodiak. "There were 23 teaching positions open in Kodiak last year," he said.

"Out of 960 applicants, we interviewed 122. We work through the placement center at the University of Alaska, attend job fairs and give half-hour interviews to prospective teachers for three days in Anchorage. We require a personal interview before we hire anyone.

"Two-week teacher orientation classes are available at the University of Alaska. The teacher placement office there, of course, tries to find jobs for their own candidates, but they will also place graduates of other colleges."

Salaries look good in Alaska. Teachers with a master's degree often begin at $35,000 and those with a master's plus 54 hours and 12 years of experience may receive about $42,000. But although these salaries seem high compared to Outside, we found them insufficient for most families. Most of the teachers we met either had moonlighting jobs or operated a fishing site during the summer. The Witteveens spent summers fishing until John got his administrative position which keeps him busy eleven months of the year.

"I doubt that I could have worked my way up as fast in the Grand Rapids school system," John said. "Here it's a shorter distance to the people who make decisions. We can deal directly with the mayor, the governor and the legislators."

And they love the life here.

"There is deer in our freezer, and the fishermen bring in halibut, crab and salmon. We keep 15 to 20 chickens and trade eggs for king crab. Fresh eggs are in demand because eggs are two months old when you get them from Outside."

"We had hunted and fished in Michigan but we had always

had a desire to come to Alaska," John added. "We'd seen travelog films, and Alaska appealed to us.

"But I wouldn't advise anyone to come here to stay without looking at it first," Tina said. "I needed good friends and we had friends to stay with when we came. Kodiak is *isolation* and you have to deal with the elements. But fewer things can get in the way of success. We like it. This is home now."

"Yes," John said, "it's true the weather is harsh, but the winters aren't usually as cold in Kodiak as in Kalamazoo."

"It's often misty and we have blowing winds and lots of rain," Tina added. "In Michigan we didn't go out into the rain much. Here we put on raincoats and go out anyway."

John said, "You need a good insulated survival suit. We carry them in our boat. You can put the suit on in the water should you capsize, and the suit can keep a person afloat and alive for as long as three or four days.

"If you come to Alaska, you should be familiar with the out-of-doors," John said. "Be a gambler type. Be a go-it-yourselfer. Tina and I built our house, doing most of the work ourselves. For six years we did little but pound nails in our spare time. Oh, yes, we also picked berries and canned salmon."

Witteveens' home in the woods is in a setting that reminded us of rain forest in the state of Washington. John and Tina often spend their weekends rabbit hunting or sailing.

Tina taught home economics before coming to Alaska but has devoted most of her time to volunteering and home activities in her new location. The couple have two children—Mark, nine and Alisa, three.

"Couples should have separate interests as well as common interests," Tina said. "If I were totally dependent on John, the weekends would be disastrous. I enjoy hobby things—like sewing. You have to like your home here, but you also have to be ready to dump everything and get out on the road to the beach when the sun shines. In Kodiak there are two choices for the road—45 miles in one direction and about

John and Kathy Witteveen

five miles in the other. When we go on the road, the kids occupy themselves on the beach with their friends while the mothers visit.

"Alaskans are more 'arty' than you'd think," Tina added. "There are theater groups in Kodiak, otherwise a movie or a high school basketball game might be all of the entertainment unless we make our own. Our Kodiak Council of the Arts brings in concert performers."

High schools are spread throughout the island although many have as few as ten or eleven students. Only one of these villages is accessible by road. John visits the others by plane or boat as part of his job as assistant superintendent.

"I make it to each of the villages twice a year for an evaluation of their program and facilities," John said. "Most areas have a primary room, secondary room, media center, gym, kitchen and library.

"If you're teaching out in one of the villages, the living is rugged and housing is difficult to find. It's real isolation. You become an advisor and have medical responsibilities in addition to teaching.

John continued, "When my father first learned we were moving to Alaska, he protested, 'But you have a job here in Michigan. Why go to Alaska?' After that Dad didn't say much, but he and Mom did come to visit us. When they were ready to go home, he quietly whispered to me, 'I guess I can see now why you moved here.'"

Rainbows and Sunsets

We first heard about Gordon Wright through Nancy Schmitt, the Press Woman whom I'd looked up in Anchorage. Nancy advised, "Talk to Gordon Wright. He's a fascinating character." She mentioned that he would be conducting the Anchorage Symphony that evening. We attended the concert.

Later I called the hotel where Gordon was staying. He agreed to meet Dave and me in the hotel lobby. From there we went to a small restaurant around the corner.

Gordon, a 48 year-old professor of music at the University of Alaska and conductor of the Fairbanks Symphony, began talking as soon as we sat down.

"Alaska has been conquered," he said. "It's all over as a frontier. There are roads now, the pipeline, orchestras, operas, theaters. Alaska was our last chance to preserve our natural heritage. But we've covered it with cement. Alaska has changed."

Gordon appeared pessimistic at first, but he revealed more optimism as he talked.

We had been impressed earlier in the new University of

Alaska auditorium as Gordon strode confidently to the podium, his long black coat tails seeming to add inches to his lean and muscular frame. The local orchestra responded to the charisma and skill of the visiting conductor by giving an excellent performance.

Tonight, sitting with us in a popular Anchorage health food restaurant, his tweed jacket and open-necked shirt were much less formal and seemed to us more appropriately collegiate—and Alaskan.

"Fairbanks was to me the end of the road," Gordon said between spoonfuls of homemade potato soup. "I was looking for an orchestra. Fairbanks was a quiet little town twelve years ago.

"My wife and three children and I arrived just before the big pipeline boom. We had sold our house in Wisconsin; I had sold my business (musical instrument sales) and we were starting all over again. The slower pace here appealed to me; there were never as many people to deal with and my schedule was less hectic.

"Things happen spontaneously in Alaska," Gordon continued, "but always in time with the harmony of the seasons. For example, when the orchestra flies into a bush village to give a concert, we're always at the mercy of the weather. In the winter they don't know when we're coming, so we just buzz the town to let them know we're there. We saw a poster in one village that said, simply, 'concert begins one hour after the orchestra arrives.'"

While his career advanced, his marriage deteriorated. Not everyone wants to wait for weather changes; and Gordon's wife chose to play the tune of her own life to the beat of a different baton. She and their children (now grown) went back Outside.

"That was my midlife crisis at age 45," he said. "I regret that I didn't handle it with more sensitivity toward others. I was driven by some force that finally erupted," he explained. "But at that time, I wasn't able to articulate the problem."

In 1978 Gordon and his wife were separated. Two years later they prepared their own $50 divorce without an attorney. Gordon said he has no regrets.

"I'm a solitary person," he repeated. "I need space. I want to live alone." He was living by himself in a simple cabin in the forested hills ten miles from his campus office. The cabin was furnished with a bunk, a table and chairs, a good wood stove and few other material possessions. There was no electricity and no plumbing.

"I want to be in control of the conveniences," Gordon explained. "I don't want them to control me. There's no telephone in the cabin, and I've learned to let the office phone at the university ring and not interrupt me when I'm having a conversation with a student or another faculty member. I guess I'm a slow learner. I don't like competition. Nobody's rushing me here. So Alaska is good for me."

He shifted to the subject of relationships. "Man was never intended to be monogamous. There's the cave man and the Christian marriage—two opposite poles with the realistic position somewhere in between."

I knew what Gordon was saying, for although I had grown up with the idea that marriage was forever, I had not been able to maintain my own first marriage. Likewise, for Gordon and his wife, as with so many couples, other things got in the way and two individuals, once headed in the same direction, no longer shared the same goals.

As a musician, Gordon found it natural to speak in musical metaphors. "Nature is harmony," he said. "Cities and people are discord. I need nature to renew myself and I need solitude to think—and to create." Yet here we sat talking with him in Anchorage, interrupting his solitude, and he seemed to be enjoying it. It was as though he had stored up ideas and needed to express them. I needed to listen.

"I wrote a symphony about nature," Gordon said, "—my "*Symphony in Ursa Major*. Now I'm composing another about technology."

Gordon Wright seems to live the best of two worlds.

Five years later when Dave and I returned to Alaska, we found Gordon Wright in Fairbanks and he brought us up to date on his life. His charisma continued to come through. He still exuded confidence and power whether he was wearing his black symphony conductor's coat or blue denim and sandals.

After seventeen years in Fairbanks as music director for the University of Alaska and conductor of the Fairbanks Symphony and the Arctic Chamber Orchestra, Gordon was preparing to move on. "I'm ready to do more free lance work," he explained. He was already doing research, writing and composing in addition to his work as music director and conductor.

It had been a challenge for Gordon to show what could be done with volunteer musicians. He met the challenge well, winning two governor's awards and receiving other honors while building and educating an Alaskan audience.

"So now I'll have more time to devote to the pursuit of music making," he said. "I expect to leave Fairbanks but remain in Alaska. I can go to my home in the Anchorage area anytime and fly non-stop almost anywhere from there. I hope to be able to do guest conducting at various locations.

"Alaska provided a good opportunity for me," he said. "I've not had to fight tradition here. Early on, my wife and I got together $2,000, chartered a plane and flew the chamber orchestra to the bush. Now these concerts have become an institution, and I no longer have to pay the expenses myself."

Gordon's musical groups have played for many people who had never listened to classical music or attended a live symphony performance.

"It has been gratifying to perform for unprejudiced audiences," Gordon said. "These people come with no preconceived notion of what an orchestra should or shouldn't be. They've been tremendously receptive!

"The initial encounter with great music is important," Gordon continued. "Our orchestra really gives of themselves always—and especially do they give in the bush."

Alaska had been a stimulating environment for Gordon. "Conducting is a solitary profession," he said. "I can't study music with other people around. I need time to myself. Now at 52, I have my social life under control," he said. "My profession and nature are compatible. I'm not interested in marrying again."

Gordon does, however, continue to maintain contact with his ex-wife.

"We agreed we'd remain friends," he said. "And I didn't

divorce my children." Gordon's two sons and daughter chose to move to Pennsylvania with their mother, who went there to work on an advanced degree in psychology.

"Alaska may be seen as a place to begin a new life," Gordon said. "But it's cold and dark in the winter. Of course there are all of the cliches about Alaska such as: Here's an opportunity to do things your own way. Here you're a big fish in a little pond. Nobody's starting rival orchestras here. We have fewer musicians here. Here one can have an urban profession and still live out his or her fantasies in a cabin in the woods.

"Unfortunately, we bring all of our personal baggage with us," Gordon added, slinging his worn and faded day pack over his shoulders.

Personal baggage. That was something to think about. Gordon wasn't referring to his backpack, of course, but to a psychological burden. I thought about what I was carrying around in my head. How much personal baggage could I really discard if I escaped to Alaska or to some other "get-away" spot?

If I was having difficulty at home making up my mind what to do about my career, would it be any easier in Alaska? Would there be any more choices here than in Michigan? I wondered. Possibly there would be fewer in Alaska. I wasn't sure.

But what about my children? Now there's a rub. I wouldn't want to leave the children Outside. I'd want to bring them with me. But what if they didn't want to come? Teenagers aren't as agreeable to moving as toddlers are. I thought the kids would have a ball up in The Great Land—lots of snow for skiing. Ice for skating and ice fishing—and hockey.

But maybe they wouldn't enjoy these activities. After all, they have their own friends at home. Just how much should parents expect from children? Would it be fair to pull them away from their friends and lifestyle, especially when we didn't have certain job prospects?

As Gordon started to leave, I asked him whether he ever tires of the primitive side of his contrasting lifestyle. Without hesitation he replied, "There are mosquitoes in Alaska—and sometimes it rains a lot. That's the price you pay for the rainbows and the sunsets."

Epilogue

January 1989

Since our first trek to Alaska, Dave and I have traveled to Great Britain, to the Soviet Union, to China, to Italy, to Hawaii, to numerous places in the continental United States and returned twice to the Arctic. But our point of departure remains our home in the Michigan woods.

Because we decided that we *could* pack up and leave (the children are older now and living away from home), we aren't sure that relocating is necessary. We can be ourselves without escaping to a new environment. We can change our lifestyle without moving. We can be flexible without uprooting ourselves. But we've ruled out nothing. We live a day, or a week, or a month at a time—trying to savor each moment. That's perhaps the most important thing I learned from listening to people who had changed their lives by moving to America's last frontier.

Index